SCIENCE MEETS ANCIENT WISDOM
TO UPLIFT LIFE ON EARTH

ENERGY JOY™

THE STRESS FIX™

BY

ROBERT SIMON SIEGEL

ENERGY JOY
THE STRESS FIX

Library of Congress Control Number: TXu 2-312-621
Library of Congress Cataloging-in-Publication Data is available on ile.

ISBN: 978-1-66787-911-6

Cover design and interior formatting
by AnitaWilliamsDesign.com

Printed in the United States of America

Printed by BookBaby
7905 N. Crescent Blvd.
Pennsauken, N.J. 08110
BookBaby.com

www.TheStressFix.com

To my parents of blessed memory:

Joan Claire Rubin and Simon Siegel,

and my ancestors.

"I allow myself to hope that the world will emerge from its present troubles, that it will one day learn to give the direction of its affairs, not to cruel swindlers and scoundrels, but to people possessed of wisdom and courage. I see before me a shining vision: a world where none are hungry, where few are ill, where work is pleasant and not excessive, where kindly feeling is common, and where minds released from fear create delight for eye, ear and heart. Do not say this is impossible. It is not impossible. I do say that it could be done... if only people would bend their minds to the achievement of the kind of happiness that should be distinctive of humanity."

— BERTRAND RUSSELL,
HUMAN SOCIETY IN ETHICS AND POLITICS (1954)

We can do this now!

"Creating a new theory is not like destroying an old barn and erecting a skyscraper in its place. It is rather like climbing a mountain, gaining new and wider views, discovering unexpected connections between our starting points and its rich environment. But the point from which we started out still exists and can be seen, although it appears smaller and forms a tiny part of our broad view gained by the mastery of the obstacles on our adventurous way up."

— ALBERT EINSTEIN

CONTENTS

To uplift we merely embrace
a science-based understanding of better
operating our phenomenal physiology
with practical 'how-to' skills.

PREFACE

Foreplay

Why Energy Joy?

It's evolution time!

A remarkable step up the evolutionary ladder is now ours to have for an extraordinary and joyous adventure. Elevating humanity into more exciting and healthier new realms begins with one intriguing discovery, known since ancient times:

> **We have an amazing energy engine inside each of us that literally generates the energy for the emotion we call joy. This is ENERGY JOY. Once we know how to turn on our ENERGY JOY engine, we can feel joy's elevating energy rush whenever we want. We can then begin gaining its remarkable evolutionary benefits that empower us to uplift life on Earth — with energy!**

In fact, how to activate this currently dormant ENERGY JOY engine and open its uplifting energy flow are the original teachings of all genuine spiritual paths, all true religions and all authentic wisdom traditions. They were all designed to accomplish this. Now we can scientifically describe more of how this works plus understand its timely immense value.

We know joy as a natural expression of the pure love of being alive. Joy uplifts our emotions, heals our body, refreshes our mind, and nourishes our entire being. Joy's valuable gifts bring improvements in health, immune strength, inspiration, attitude, relationships and the feel-good neurotransmitters for greater enjoyment of life. Clearly, joy is healthy. That's because...

Joy is the energy of health.

But joy is elusive for most people. Joy happens all too rarely and only serendipitously. Fortunately, that changes once we know how to make this inner connection. Joy's elevating energy rush is then available — anytime we want.

Beyond a brief emotional uplift, precious though that is, the benefits of feeling joy may, in fact, be THE most vital ingredient for further human development. This is because joy is a connection *within* ourself that opens the flow of a very special energy. As if giving us a reward that guides us to grow, the energy of joy also activates new human capabilities we have not yet discovered, but have been known since ancient times.

Turning on our ENERGY JOY engine is an acquired competency. This competency, in the form of body/mind skills, is also the original content of all true spiritual paths, all genuine religions and all authentic wisdom traditions. The wisest humans throughout history knew the value of gaining access to this special energy flow. All traditions had their own poetic coded names and hidden metaphors for this, because the techniques had to be kept secret throughout millennia. Humans were not yet ready.

Ready or not, it's become a necessity.

Fortuitously, these skills simultaneously fix stress.

Ancient wisdom traditions, long ago, developed practical techniques to achieve a tuning up of our body/mind which they called 'spiritual enlightenment'. I call it ENERGY JOY because one does not have to be a saint or even a spiritual seeker to achieve the uplifting awareness that practicing these techniques for ENERGY JOY will bring.

In these pages, I will walk you through the simple steps to learn how to operate your human physiology—your body/mind—in ways that directly ignite your ENERGY JOY engine and bring into you its elevating energy flow we experience as the emotion of joy.

This book will show you how to access your own ENERGY JOY in any given moment and why it matters to know this ability.

Facing Reality

A phenomenal evolutionary leap is ours, if... we choose to uplift life on Earth. But a first step for any solution is to acknowledge the problem. Only when we face biological reality with brutal honesty will we ever enjoy our shared species-wide longings for global peace, prosperity and health.

The relationship we now have with biological reality is so dangerously flawed with idiocy that we actually reward those who destroy, contaminate and pollute the very sources necessary for biological life. Over time, we have been convinced to make, sell and pay for things that destroy our own habitat. This is neither sustainable nor a sign of intelligence.

Practically speaking, to uplift means we need to fix the driver of our global economic reward system so it promotes health and joy. As we shall see, these two fundamental values best align our human species with biological reality and together steer global civilization into real prosperity.

And if we don't uplift?

Our human species will soon go the way of all extinct life forms who never figured out a most basic truth: how to contribute enough value to biological life to be ecologically essential. This is the only real 'survival of the fittest'.

While going about our daily stress-filled lives, too few of us are aware that our very survival is at stake. Since it doesn't make the news, it doesn't seem real or urgent. So instead we feel a constant 'free floating' anxiety, but without identifying its cause or its purpose. Stress is a natural, biological warning signal to correct our course.

While we won't know exactly when — until it's too late — it is very likely that if we continue on our current path, we shall activate the survival instinct of all the other species whose habitats we are destroying.

They will naturally join forces to remove their common threat: humans. Imagine a hundred wildly mutating, lethal viruses unleashed all at once.

The guiding values of health and joy, so simple yet so profoundly functional, are needed to replace six ruinous myths that lock humanity into an invisible prison. Like a glass ceiling, this prison prevents our advancing and now threatens our existence. By articulating these myths, we can better question their usefulness and their validity in order to upgrade them. This is like a standard process in psychotherapy that effectively helps individuals become free of false beliefs, usually from childhood traumas that limit their lives. We need to do this now at a species level.

Myth #1: Humans are a fully developed species with no further evolution absolutely necessary to continue our survival.

Myth #2: Stress is only a useless, irritating prehistoric 'fight or flight' survival reaction with no valuable evolutionary purpose to humans now.

Myth #3: The current global economic reward system is the best way to enable people to create value, innovate, cooperate and improve life.

Myth #4: *We the People of the Earth* together cannot possibly establish healthy global sanity that triumphs over the control freaks in business, government and technology without force, money or massive media ownership.

Myth #5: Microwaving the planet with 5G, cellphone towers and telecommunications satellites has nothing to do with global increases in cancers, auto-immune diseases or dementia and cannot be changed to support biological health.

Myth #6: Ancient wisdom of how to live well on Earth has no value. Therefore today's peoples are the most advanced humans, and pharmaceutically managing (but never curing) preventable pollution-caused diseases is superior to growing super-healthy ecological environments that produce healthier people.

Replacing these myths with biological reality will swiftly elevate humanity into exciting and healthier new realms. But because cajoling those who don't want change may take more than time, *We the People of the Earth* can activate our uplifting at a more foundational level in ways we shall discover are quite powerful. We grow the energy that nourishes life. This elevation process is the goal of my book.

Rewards of Joy

Turning on this ENERGY JOY engine inside us feels so wonderful because that 'good' feeling is designed to guide us to want more and more, until... we activate our biological intelligence. This is our essential human life guidance system. It is how we best evolve.

Alarmingly, as a civilization, our access to this vital connection within ourselves has been eclipsed, bordering on atrophy; and so we find ourselves dangerously misaligned with biological reality. Ever more wasteful of precious life is that we have been unable to enjoy this ecstatic state and use it as the platform for elevating all our interactions.

Our education as a species demands that we earn our joy. It requires learning lessons so we advance.

It's a no-brainer that we need to reverse the sad state of human affairs around the world. Our necessity is to swiftly halt accelerating downward spirals of disease, environmental destruction, biological and nuclear weapon races, massive population displacement and profit-driven pollution of all known sources required for biological life.

So far, we have yet to embrace the most basic fact of reality: value the health of our biosphere and serve life by nourishing its health — or else lose it. Common-sense safeguards are needed in all these areas, but they do not by themselves grow a better, wiser human being.

ENERGY JOY does.

We now need ENERGY JOY to repair the devastation of our human psyche from the burdensome emotional impacts of current events.

This undermining has resulted in world-wide chronic stress damage. Our entire species must fix stress; it's very doable.

If something simple such as a set of seven body/mind skills could rapidly reverse this downward trajectory, it is worth giving it a go.

We can ignite the engine of ENERGY JOY with body/mind skills that also fix stress easily by better operating our four major body systems: Central Nervous System, Sympathetic Nervous System, Parasympathetic Nervous System and Skeletal Muscle System. Then we can rapidly move out of the dangerous disease development process underlying countless illness conditions and ignorance that we so casually refer to as "stressed out."

Fixing stress first is precisely how we activate our biological intelligence and operate our life guidance system.

To accomplish this, we simply flip each of these four body systems into their health-generating 'treasure mode', instead of keeping them stuck in their disease-causing modes that generate the damaging symptoms and illnesses of stress. This can be done in seconds with the body/mind skills in this book. The result is 'Dynamic Calm'.

Together these four body systems can then provide even greater benefits. They can elevate our HPA-axis, the hypothalamus/pituitary/adrenal gland mechanism. The HPA-axis is our stress damage factory. It's also our 'awareness control center' which determines whether our relationship with the world is healthy or not. Our control center is now 'stressed out' of control. But we can easily fix our HPA-axis by tuning it to uplift and generate far more fascinating, useful capabilities.

The minimal effort required to take the steps to create ENERGY JOY is spelled out in this book. They will refresh how we observe life and operate in the world. This may appear to be a formidable task, but it isn't.

> **We merely embrace a science-based understanding of better operating our phenomenal physiology with practical 'how-to' skills to uplift.**

There are only seven skills needed to fix stress and uplift. Once learned, the first five merge into one. Ultimately, they all become one to form a healthy, elegant way of being.

Shifting our species' priorities to uplift life on Earth is as huge as was discovering fire, and vastly more important than recognizing that the Earth revolves around the Sun. Achieving this uplift will be enormously more exciting, richly more rewarding and far more fun than staying stuck in survival's quagmire.

ENERGY JOY feels wonderful and will make you feel more alive because you will have more life-force energy flowing through you. Yet as valuable as ENERGY JOY is to us individually, it is fantastically more functional to us as a species.

For reasons described in this book, ENERGY JOY is likely the most valuable gift that our species is here to contribute and enjoy. It leads to fulfillment of our true magnificent human potential on Earth. Just like plants grow from seeds into their fruit-blossoming maturity, our human species has four more stages of growth yet to achieve. Each is enormously better than its predecessor, and each produces greater life-enhancing fruit.

With ENERGY JOY, we begin elevating. We cannot yet imagine the good that awaits.

However, to activate the extraordinary adventure before us, we have an interesting global challenge. We need to generate enough ENERGY JOY to achieve the energetic tipping point that uplifts humanity into a far grander existence — so we leave survival's stupor. But... because we don't know how many of us it will take, it's 'all hands on deck'.

The tools and understandings to claim your personal treasures, your biological heritage and to activate our UPLIFTING are what this book provides for you.

Re-reading may reveal new insights that, like seeds, help grow your awareness. As you engage, you may find that this book is alive!

The Author's Wish

Steering a new direction out of today's challenging chaos, ENERGY JOY shows how science and physiology can better operate together with all things 'energy' as a greater whole with a singular purpose: to uplift our human species and life on Earth. The results we achieve are the original treasured goals of every authentic spiritual path, every true religion and every genuine wisdom tradition. It's time to recognize, value and embrace wisdom.

In the process, we easily fix stress — for good — by understanding what stress really is, by applying ancient skills that science and physiology can now describe, and by thus achieving its amazing evolutionary purpose that activates our missing biological intelligence. Doing this elevates our consciousness into a vastly more rewarding partnership with life on Earth.

I have done my utmost to learn and share what I believe are the essential foundations for this natural quest to uplift. As humans we are endowed with fantastic capabilities that await our discovery. While a few exceptional individuals throughout human history have achieved their personal 'uplift', our entire human species is now ripe to uplift.

Once enough of us crack the code to turn on the dormant but wondrous ENERGY JOY engine inside us, which has always been the secret heart of our spiritual/religious/wisdom traditions, then all heaven can break loose!

My goal is to present the essential ancient wisdom skills that enable us — *We the People of the Earth* — to together activate our UPLIFTING and do so now. The greatest adventure of human evolution is open before us.

UPLIFTING of humanity can happen swiftly because it is done with energy, a more foundational realm of our physical reality. It is like we are turning life more 'ON'. The awareness we can grow with ENERGY JOY celebrates our relationship with biological life. Ultimately, we gain what I call 'Eco-Joy' – communicating with other species as indigenous peoples around the world have been doing for millennia.

These skills and understandings have been forty years in development throughout my personal and professional journey. By needing to triumph over phobic type panic attacks from a college public speaking debacle, I was highly motivated to identify the body systems involved in stress, anxiety and panic. One-by-one I developed skills that restore healthy functioning to each of these major body systems in seconds, without pills, so that I could enjoy public speaking. I found that I was then able to help hundreds of people with a vast variety of stress-induced problems of mind and body in hospitals, medical clinics, wellness centers and corporate trainings. I now believe these skills should be taught to all people, especially to our children in schools.

Throughout my professional life, I was always simultaneously engaged in intense personal trainings with lineage-holders of wisdom traditions – people thought of as 'masters' and 'enlightened' beings. My goal was both to develop myself in the spiritual realms and to bring that specialized knowledge into science and physiology so that people could benefit from learning how our body, mind and energy can optimally operate. I never suspected that it would take over four decades to connect the dots.

In aligning science with ancient wisdom, it is fascinating to understand that before modern physics terms were invented, some of the words we associate with spiritual and religious terms refer to actual 'substance' – which could only be conveyed with poetic allusions. Those highly coded instructions were remarkably specific and were designed to operate as a multi-dimensional science at levels we are not yet aware.

That original science teaches how to develop a human being into a far more advanced being. Our awareness grows by connecting with what opens the flow of this special energy inside us. Thankfully, as an enticing reward, it activates this energy source of our prized emotion of joy.

ENERGY JOY informs us of Life's benevolence.

Now we can describe these goings on with modern physics terms, especially the newly emerging field of bio-physics. The result is 'energy health', a higher level of wellness.

I hope this is intriguing enough to entice you to fully explore and apply the content of ENERGY JOY. I predict you will benefit in new and surprisingly uplifting ways. And if we indeed activate the uplifting of life on Earth, we get to play in a most extraordinary adventure.

Wishing you ENERGY JOY's treasures,

Robert Simon Siegel, MS

INTRODUCTION

The Five Dots of Reality to Connect

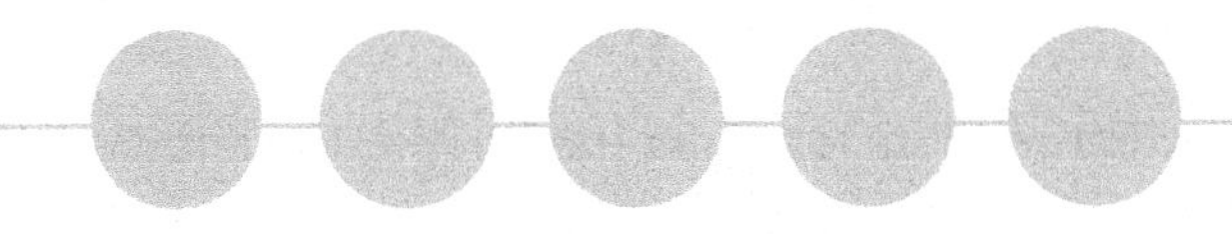

Dots love to connect. That's what they do.

A good thing to know is that when dots connect, they have dot joy. So they love to connect. The more the merrier.

Dots also go for a bigger experience. Their natural drive and the juicy dot fuel they love, is to connect all the dots needed to be their greater dot — the whole greater than the sum of their dots. More than anything, this gives them a really gigantic multi-dot 'joygasm', because they want the greater joys of being their greater whole.

From the tiniest electrons and cells to human communities and our global ecosystem, life's things seem to like to connect to form greater wholes. This evolutionary direction grows all life to be increasingly healthier parts of increasingly greater wholes. Making wholes non-functional by disconnecting their parts goes backward in evolution.

We humans also have a greater whole. Being our greater whole uplifts us into amazing new levels of joy. As we grow this coherence, we gain a most valuable reward, long considered 'The Prize'. We gain access to the greater intelligence of our greater whole.

We have a long-awaited, species-wide uplift before us. Our uplift has been thirteen billion years in the making. To have this species-wide joy, we must connect five dots of our biological reality.

Science has now recognized these five dots of reality. However, only ancient wisdom has the knowledge to connect them to activate the functioning of their greater whole.

Ancient wisdom also has the WHY — the knowledge of its value.

It's time for all human activities to re-organize around what's most important and most valuable for healthy biological life. Then we can discover truly new life-nourishing ways we need to uplift out of our current quagmire, so that we can produce an optimally healthy population and enjoy living in an optimally healthy planet.

All the other species of Earth are nourishing life — all of them. It's our turn. We humans need to learn how to nourish life, immediately and thoroughly. So we are going to connect the dots of reality.

> **When we connect these dots of reality, we reset life on Earth into uplifting.**

What five important dots of reality are humans to connect to uplift?

Meet the Dots of Reality!

REALITY DOT #1: What Is Inside You

You have an amazing energy engine built into your physiology. Every human being has this energy engine.

But it is dormant.

Only a very few people throughout our human history have figured out how to activate and operate this energy engine. These we have called the wise, sages, holy people, prophets, lovers of life and exceptional individuals who have made magnificent contributions to humanity.

We are all here to turn on this energy engine — NOW — and receive its treasures. It's how we uplift ourselves and uplift life on Earth.

What treasures? Even though it is dormant, this engine is still the energy source of our two most valued emotions: joy and love. Imagine it fully activated.

How important is this energy engine? It's THE prize of life. Joy inspires every aspect of life. Turning on this energy engine is the very foundation — the original goal — of every genuine religion, every authentic spiritual path and every true wisdom tradition.

Why? Because it increasingly opens the flow of something exceedingly precious.

What? From where to where?

This is the great mystery of wisdom. Those who attempt to describe it can only use poetry and metaphor, because words cannot equal the deliciousness of the real experience.

In a sense, it activates your higher energy or 'spiritual' DNA. Those who taste, know.

REALITY DOT #2: What We Are

We humans are ourselves a next generation of biological life. We are a type of flowering plant, a hybrid of physical and non-physical. At our best, we grow an uplifting, expansive awareness that is no longer restricted to our five physical senses.

We call this 'spiritual'. But it is just becoming more conscious of what we actually are.

Our fruit, our blossom, is an amazing energy that nourishes life itself.

We are here to contribute this energy fertilizer by opening the flow from its elevated non-physical source into the physicality of our biosphere — our Earth Mother.

Some may call it evolution. But long ago human seeds were planted to grow. As a human, we are a special kind of seed.

The amazing energy that we can grow increasingly turns the biosphere of our Earth Mother into a paradise beyond our current imagination. This is our birthright.

But it is also our responsibility.

We grow this nourishing, uplifting energy by learning how to focus in an ancient way that grows our awareness of what we are, developed by earlier humans who had far more advanced awareness — and far more purity of benevolent motivation — than have we.

The time is ripe for us to blossom our energy fruit. As soon as we do, we uplift.

Science can now describe many aspects of this. And so it shall in this book.

Because we have dots to connect.

REALITY DOT #3:
Where We Are

Like a plant's first bud to blossom, is Earth — life's only biologically alive planet to be found so far within billions of light years across countless galaxies, each with billions of suns and tens of billions of planets.*

A complete rarity in time, space and spirit, Earth is THE precious living gem of the entire universe.

Bursting with new energy for being alive, the joyous awakening of Spring is celebrated by all of Nature's creatures — birds, bees, plants, animals and humans. Spring's exuberance offers a tiny taste of what is coming our way when we start uplifting.

Our human flowering on Earth has been 13 billion years in the making. That is 13,000,000,000 years. We human beings have emerged within this living planet's biosphere thanks to a magnificent symphony of flora and fauna. Our life is made possible only because all other species cooperate, collaborate and contribute to nourishing biological life.[1]

---

* The vast distance between Earth and even the nearest stars means that the light we see from them, by the time it reaches us, is millions of years old and older. This means that there indeed could be many other biologically active and developed planets by now.

If this universe were a tourist destination, Earth would be the prize, the most fantastic recreational playground of unmatched physical beauty anywhere in the entire universe.

Our planet is the place to be! And we are here — as a human species of being!

Earth is the Garden of Eden, 'Gan Eden' as called in its original Hebrew in the Torah's first chapter of Genesis. This translates literally as 'Garden of Delights'.

Why?

REALITY DOT #4: What Our Earth Mother Does

Our Earth Mother grows things! Is that not incredible?

Unlike all the planets we've viewed across the known universe, we live in an amazing world where things grow. Biological life grows everywhere all by itself! When we want food and flowers, we simply plant seeds and they sprout into delicious, nutritious edibles, plant medicines and living beauty.

Yet there is something even more fantastic here.

This amazing world also grows our thoughts into things!

You focus on a goal. Somehow, you learn to do the actions which fertilize your desire into being, and you manifest your intention into physical reality — from nothing but a thought.

While it doesn't always happen in one instant, to make anything physical out of a thought is extraordinarily magical. The slowness makes it seem natural and normal. But when it happens faster, we consider it miraculous. Same process.

Just as a seed has its potential already built in, awaiting activation, so our best ideas and best desires have potential — needing only activation from our focus.

This works because of our Earth Mother's prized secret. Best-kept from unripe humans, bio-physics can now describe it as a quality of our living reality.

Our focus directs energy.

Comprehending this is now the single most important thing we humans need to do.

Why?

Without such comprehension, our species' focus is now creating severe planetary destruction, disease and imprisonment within deteriorating possibilities for survival. This downward life spiral resembles the draining of a bathtub, but taking us and many other life forms with it.

Because we do not focus properly, we are currently a most dysfunctional species. We do not yet understand what it means that focus directs energy, nor why it is key to the very nature of reality.

We have yet to consider the possibilities of focusing to create our best reality.

The problem is that some humans are still fighting to conquer everyone and everything in an ancient war of biological survival that our species has already won millennia ago. We now know how to survive. We can easily grow food and build shelter. And so instead of blossoming boundless biological beauty, these misguided people are contaminating the very sources of biological life itself.

Why do *We the People of the Earth* allow such suicidal idiocy?

While that by itself is remarkably stupid, an entirely uncharted new level of human stupidity is having a global economic system that rewards those who contaminate and destroy the very sources of all biological life.

It is exactly opposite to the most basic goal of biological life that makes everything healthy and enjoyable. This is simply to nourish life. Never pollute. No other species pollutes.

We have only a small window of time to join all other species that cooperate, collaborate and contribute to nourishing biological life. If we do not, two eventualities will result. One is that we destroy ourselves by ruining all the essential sources of biological life we ourselves need to live.

More likely, before that happens, the other species on Earth will be forced into activating their own survival instincts and will cooperate, collaborate and contribute to defend their habitats and eliminate their common enemy: humans.

Has this already begun?

After witnessing the global devastation to human civilization from a single virus, it is easy to imagine a lethal and wildly mutating, multi-species, concerted multi-virus effort.

All species want the same thing: to celebrate life by playing in healthy planetary joy. Except for those dysfunctional humans making money by polluting, contaminating and designing life-destroying weapons, real people everywhere prefer living in a healthy Nature.

All humans should be on board with nourishing life. Why?

We are designed to enjoy vibrant well-being — together. It's not 'us' against 'them. It's all 'us'. As a family of biological beings, unique in the universe, we're all in the business of moving health and joy up into their greater wholes. This planet is far too rare and precious to disrespect or take for granted.

Effectively directing our species' focus is our next step that moves us up the evolutionary ladder. Science would call it an evolutionary possibility.

Wisdom traditions call it our destination. Wisdom traditions have long ago figured out the 'code'. They share a vision of how to best live in our Earth Mother. Indigenous peoples of the Earth already know how to live and play in planetary joy. Yet so many were destroyed as 'uncivilized' by those with less evolved biological intelligence and biologically inferior values.

What happens when you begin to feel the fantastically loving, generously giving being that is our Earth Mother — her energy, her spirit, her soul? Indigenous peoples know this.

You fall in love.

How could you not? When we nourish biological life, our Earth Mother grows even more extraordinary things.

As you begin to have fun encounters and interesting experiences with other species, your mind widens into recognizing the wondrous beauty of the living, conscious being we call Nature. We have yet to evolve an entirely new realm of communicating — actual exchanging of thoughts — with the other creatures on Earth. This uplifting we gain from joining the community of living beings is Eco-Joy.

What is our potential? What activates us? What should we be focusing on, intending, desiring & energizing? Always remember:

Our Earth Mother grows things! Choose your thought seeds wisely.

Let us now begin our species' uplift.

REALITY DOT #5: What We Are Here To Do

We are here to focus our attention in ways that grow the amazing, uplifting energy that activates paradise on Earth — the essential 'Energy of Life'. This achievement has always been THE goal at the foundation of all genuine religions, all true spiritual paths and all intact wisdom traditions.

We activate this flow by turning on the ENERGY JOY engine inside us.

By opening this flow, we are actually doing something extraordinary and wondrous. We are connecting realms — the physical and the 'spiritual'. We are uniting that which ancient wisdom traditions call 'heaven and earth'.

As an enticing prelude, when we do focus to open this flow of life energy, we experience uplifting sensations we recognize as joy, love, soothing calm and an inexplicable sense of well-being. This is our guidance system at work, rewarding us to evolve.

As humans, this special energy first fills our bodies, invigorating and uplifting all of our cells, tissues, organs and glands into entirely new levels of optimal health. Then it flows into the environment around us. Our interactions with others seem to naturally uplift into mutual benefit. We somehow attract more of what we want in life. We feel more alive.

This is because we are growing a mutually rewarding, interactive friendship with 'reality'. Why fight reality when we can communicate and successfully partner with it? We want a mutually beneficial relationship with reality.

As our abilities develop, we overflow this energy into the conscious, living energy matrix that constantly forms and sustains all matter on Earth. This greater whole of our biosphere is its energy-organizing structure that physics might call Earth's 'quantum field'. When enough of us do this, a tipping point will be achieved, and we signal the living energy matrix to open its 'pores' to allow much more of the treasures this special fertilizer of life delivers into our physical reality.

We want to saturate our biosphere with the human fruit, the Energy of Life that is ENERGY JOY.

As a species we are applying the ancient 'Law of Attraction'. By applying our focus, we direct energy. Together we uplift. Life on Earth can then change for the better – enormously so.

This shows this conscious living energy matrix of our Earth Mother that we have matured as a species, that we are done with survival's petty squabbles from our species' babyhood, and we are ready to invite what can only be called 'THE UPLIFTING'.

This is what we are here to activate.

What is 'THE UPLIFTING'?

Beyond the physical, we are uplifting into bigger, better consciousness by directly engaging the 'Energy of Life'. To fathom such an expansion, we can apply a brilliant and valuable wisdom tool that will help us learn to translate what we know – the physical – into what we now need to know – its energy level counterparts.

Since the physical comes from the energetic, our understanding will not be perfect. But... we hugely benefit from knowing how things flourish in the physical realm to sense what flourishes in the energetic realm. Flourishing at all levels is our path.

> This wisdom tool is:
> **"As above, so below; as within, so without."**

Like healthy soil sprouts the abundant plant life that nourishes all other creatures, a healthy quantum field is the energy level soil that grows the fabric of reality itself. It does so in the most magnificent and delightfully wondrous ways we have yet to even imagine. This is what we — our human species — are here to activate. It's our contribution and our purpose.

It is our special honor and privilege to do.

All other living species of 'peoples' of Earth — the plants, animals, birds, fish, insects, stones and the elements of water, air, earth and fire — are depending on us to do our job. They are waiting for us to wake up and join the community of sentient living beings.

We must succeed. We cannot fail.

It is now time for our species to uplift life on Earth, and stop our species' further destruction of precious biological life that has taken so many eons to develop.

Why do we want to do this?

We have a bigger, much better wave to ride and a most incredible game of evolution itself to win. This wave is the most exciting adventure of Creation's thirteen billion years. It now beckons us strongly because... it is already here, ready for us to ride. We ride this wave by turning on our energy engine.

What is this game-changing energy engine we seek to activate?

Just as the rays of sunshine from the physical sun of our solar system nourish all biological life on Earth, we radiate something so extraordinary that it is called 'ENERGY JOY'.

Like the beautiful sweetness a nursing mother gives her child, when it is turned on and activated, your ENERGY JOY engine delivers the very energy that loves life into its fullness of being. It does so from within you.

This is why we feel joy and love.

This energy of joy is the treasure of life itself. So phenomenal is its effect that it delivers the energy essence of what we poetically call 'divine' and 'blessings'. It is what makes us our healthiest, our most joyous, our most wise and our most benevolent. How it does that is what this book is about.

ENERGY JOY can uplift us and uplift life on Earth to our next, more advanced evolutionary destination. We are quantum leaping.

This growth turns on and restores our vitalizing human experience of that which is truly sacred, precious, joyous and holy about life on Earth. As our ENERGY JOY engine radiates, it further activates the energy of life within each living thing. This aliveness, that is poetically called the 'divine spark', blossoms.

The real beauty of 'Sleeping Beauty' awakens.

We can more fully experience and comprehend even more of the amazing reality of our wondrously miraculous home here on Earth.

Imagine a planetary, species-wide celebration of our success!

But… how do we go about connecting these dots? If only a very few people throughout human history have managed to turn on this amazing energy engine, how can we hope to achieve this?

Are there instructions? Do we have guidance? Clues? What must we do differently with our body, mind and energy? How do we turn on our Energy Joy engine?

Fortunately, there is a single answer to all these questions.

WE FIX STRESS!

PART I:

OUR SIGNALS TO UPLIFT

Stress has a missing better half.
Properly understood, stress functions
as our evolutionary vehicle.

1

WHAT IS STRESS REALLY?

Stress is not what you think. It's not what you've been told. Even physicians, psychiatrists and psychologists don't know what stress is.

Why?

They have not connected the five dots of reality that place stress within its actual context. They have also not applied the wisdom tool: *as above, so below; as within, so without*. Stress is but a part of a far greater whole. Without awareness of its whole, tinkering with 'managing' that as a separate part cannot solve stress.

Connecting the five dots elevates stress into its proper place, which is absolutely amazing. It makes the purpose of stress completely clear and immensely valuable. It transforms our awareness of the physiology of stress into appreciating its beautiful symphony of exquisite precision and phenomenal benevolence that connects us to — and gives us the keys to positively influence — reality itself.

And... it makes stress damage quite easy to fix. Here we go!

What is stress?

Stress is a signal, a very special signal. Stress is an 'awareness signal' that signals us through our body to become more aware — immediately — in the present moment. It serves to tune us into a specific stream of time where time itself is most alive and has greater purpose. This signal connects us to where life actually lives.

The signal of stress opens a sort of portal, where time can deliver special goods to us.

Of what?

Awareness. A much greater awareness than our five physical senses can bring.

For what purpose?

> **To receive a communication.**

Throughout our entire range of human behavior, from basic physical survival to the highest realms of consciousness and intuition, stress delivers messages for us to change in some way that improves our lives.

> **This life guidance called 'stress' is our biological intelligence at work. Stress is an 'opportunity awareness signal' that signals us to become aware of opportunities to uplift — at every level. For humans, it is our evolutionary vehicle.**

As an awareness signal, stress interrupts our focusing to alert us to a full range of life's opportunities: to survive, defend, create, feel joy, adapt successfully, live our best values, to love life, laugh and to evolve.

At its most basic, stress is known to trigger the 'fight or flight' survival reaction. Strangely, the medical model stopped there in its understanding.

Even then, stress signals opportunities to live longer by mobilizing our energy and focus to fight or flee for our lives. This threesome of energy, focus and mobility provides the uplifting fuel that rides with all its opportunities.

Most intriguingly, as an awareness signal, this means:

> **The mysterious source of this stress signal is far more aware than we are.**

Herein begins the connecting of the dots — because when we do, we open fuller access to that source. And... we definitely want a better relationship with that more aware source.

> **Developing a relationship with that source is our evolutionary journey.**

What we have called 'stress' is but the signaling element of a much larger structure, an exquisite mechanism built into us. Like fitting all the pieces of a puzzle together to finally see the entire picture, when we connect the dots correctly, a most marvelous revelation blossoms.

We begin to fathom 'what's what'. WHAT'S the most valuable thing we can do and WHAT we really are.

Naturally, like all living organisms, we have a biological 'processor' that literally tunes us to be aware of reality. It is this processor that has allowed our human species to rise above the herds of animals and creatures. But the ignorance and misuse of this processor has now made us dangerous to all biological life.

As a two-sided coin of blessing and curse, our biological processor has been stuck for millennia exclusively on mere survival, with rare exceptions. Our grand 'opportunity awareness signal' — that could be uplifting us immensely — has only been delivering communications that restrict our focus onto survival issues with fight or flight reactions.

Our entire awareness, the whole of what we've been conscious of, is still basic surviving. Nothing more. Our limited ability to focus and pay attention has been full — only — of the stuff of survival: anger, fear, problems, worries, dangers, enemies and difficulties. Virtually all of our social, political, psychological and economic endeavors are about merely surviving.

Nothing more ambitious.

It's like settling for crumbs when a four-course gourmet meal is available.

Before our restrictive survival mentality destroys us, we must now quickly flip this imbalance into the hugely more valuable awareness for uplifting. To enjoy the full palate of its delicious delicacies, we simply fix stress at each of its four stages or levels. Each progressively nourishes and expands our 'being' until we reach the very sweetest dessert of being a human on Earth.

What happens when your stress is fixed?

2

WHEN YOU FIX YOUR STRESS

When you fix your stress, you enter the jet stream current of 'uplifting' far beyond mere survival.

The wisdom tool — *as above, so below; as within, so without* — means that just as there is a physical realm jet stream current of air in the atmosphere and fast currents of water in the ocean, there is also one for our evolution.

When you ride this wave, you uplift your mind, your body, your health, your immune system, your emotions, your energy, your relationships, your consciousness and your being. You join the greater community of living beings on Earth. It's a package deal!

You become what ancient wisdom traditions call a 'real human being'.

The rather recent application of quantum physics to understanding biology, called quantum biology or bio-physics, has terms for this elevation. ('Quantum' refers to the smallest packet or unit of energy.) As a living system you transition or phase shift into more coherent and dynamic macroscopic order.[2] This macrophasic shift simply means that from being a rather isolated fragmented part, you join a greater whole. 'Learning' is an example of this same shift.

> ***When your stress is fixed,* you easily prevent stress symptoms, illnesses and diseases — for life. You can eliminate stress damage, not merely 'manage' stress.**

You become free of stress damage because you are able to feel calm and be focused within six seconds — while moving, working, driving or computing. This stops unhealthy survival reactions of stress before any symptoms or disease can develop — which prevents a vast majority of all primary care doctor visits [3,4,5] and sick days [6,7,8] at work.

One very relevant result is that you can easily turn off the physiology of fear, which liberates your mind to better perceive solutions, opportunities and creative possibilities.

Enjoying this valuable health skill called 'Dynamic Calm' [9], extra abilities join the uplift.

> ***When your stress is fixed,* you gain health treasures.**

Within six seconds, you can activate your optimal health treasures by flipping your four major body systems away from producing virtually all stress symptoms. Your Central Nervous System, Sympathetic Nervous System, Skeletal Muscle System and Para-Sympathetic Nervous System all become health-producers. The resulting four health treasures — Presence of Mind, Emotional Calm, Physical Relaxation & Inner Peace — further align together into a greater whole of health that heals, rejuvenates and energizes. You have a new, healthier platform for 'being' in the world!

By aligning these four body systems together, your body does something amazing.

> **Within seconds you enter the ancient prized body/mind state called 'meditation'.**

One reason this ancient state is so treasured throughout history around the world is that when in this state, you enjoy greatly improved access to the source of your creativity, your intuition and your inner guidance. From this healthy body/mind state, you can more easily and accurately perceive the communications of your opportunity awareness signal.

You 'tune in' and can better ride the waves that are for uplifting — for guiding your life.

With your four major body systems operating together in their 'treasure mode', you more easily activate a fifth major system and gain its exquisite treasure: Uplifting Energy.

> ***When your stress is fixed,* your ENERGY JOY engine turns on and radiates its energy fruit. This is the energy source of joy. You replace stress with joy.**

The goal is to turn on this wonderful treasure — ENERGY JOY — so you can feel joy whenever you want with energy. Instead of the survival realm energy of adrenalin, you fill your body and your energy field with uplifting ENERGY JOY. Bio-physics is now able to describe how this means you are rejuvenating, healing and nourishing the communication between all of your trillions of cells for new levels of optimal health.

> ***When your stress is fixed,* you activate your true biological intelligence: 'Eco-Joy'.**

By radiating a field of ENERGY JOY, plants and all of Nature sense that you are safe and desirable to exchange energy with. Like indigenous peoples have enjoyed for millennia, you can experience a heart-nourishing adventure of delightful inter-species communications called 'Eco-Joy'. You join Nature. Other species have fantastic stories to tell you. They may share their wisdom, humor and joy.

> ***When your stress is fixed,* you have a direct way of communicating to the living energy matrix of our biosphere, which we can consider as the beautiful mind of our Earth Mother.**

Like streamlined prayer, you can utilize what is your 'Genius Focus'[10] to direct your energy into what physics would call the Earth's 'quantum field'. This is how to communicate your intentions and receive more of what you want, while naturally boosting your immune strength with its use. As a species, we can then utilize the benevolent nature of reality to enjoy living in this, the most magnificent recreational playground in the entire universe.

All these valuable benefits are yours simply by restoring health to a single mechanism in your body. Operating this single mechanism is what fixes your stress — for life — and activates your uplifting.

I would like to introduce you to this mechanism, your 'biological processor'.

3

BIOLOGICAL INTELLIGENCE

Your HPA-Axis

Awareness is our core operating system. If you're not aware, what are you? More importantly, when you're not aware, WHEN are you? WHEN in time are you based when you are not being aware in the present? That would be good to know.

What determines your awareness is WHEN in time you are focusing. If you're not based in the present, the timing of life, you cannot uplift. Because the present is the living portal into greater and greater awareness.

> **The more you are aware in the present, the more connected you are with reality.**

Why do you think we have awareness? What are its functions? Most importantly, what are its possibilities? These we shall explore.

But awareness is not simply seeing, hearing, smelling, tasting and feeling. The main purposes of awareness are to judge. And react.

> **Awareness has exquisite purpose — to signal us to interact with life in ways that keep us healthy and improve our relationship with reality.**

The prized goal of awareness is being 'in the flow' – where we just seem to be in the right place at the right time. We don't need opportunity awareness signals because we're already tuned in. We are riding the living wave.

Our awareness signaling comes with a powerful filtering process that determines – and signals us – if something is right or wrong, true or false and good or bad. Upgrading this filter is ultimately what moves us out of mere survival – as individuals and as a species. In a way, it is ultimately what psychology aims to achieve.

Meet your biological processor! Your HPA-axis.

Your HPA-axis is the judge, jury and executioner of your awareness.[11] This fascinating three-gland partnership consists of your hypothalamus, pituitary and adrenal glands. It is the physiological mechanism that runs our reality and is our stress factory. Without knowing how to operate it, we are constantly creating stress damage, making us capable of destroying ourselves and the environment.

Without knowing how to operate our HPA-axis, we lack biological intelligence.

The experience of stress means our HPA-axis has already decided that something we are experiencing is bad, false or wrong. It means we've begun reacting with a bodily survival response, that if unchecked will quickly spread into our emotions, our thinking and our motivation. At every level it creates increasing devastation – symptoms, immune weakness, illness and disease. That is why we must learn how to operate it.

Judging everything with survival in mind has been our default mode, like having a red filter over our perceptual lens. Everything is seen and reacted to first as a potential red-alert problem. This survival filter is unhealthy, because it keeps our HPA-axis in its stress damage mode. To uplift, we want to change this and add healthier options.

HPA-Axis

Operating Our Evolution Vehicle

Our HPA-axis is our biological processor that attunes us to reality. Its four main functions help us to sense, judge, react and repeat as required to achieve our species' evolution goals via our dominant value:

1. **signal perception** – from both our external and internal environments
2. **evaluation** – whether good/bad, right/wrong, true/false
3. **reaction** – uplift for growth or defend for survival
4. **awareness focus** – opportunity or danger

The physiological consequences are either illness-developing or health-generating. This is why we need skills to easily move our four main body systems, our focus and our energy source away from stress – altogether – and uplift into the body/mind/energy state of joy. A healthy HPA-axis evolves us.

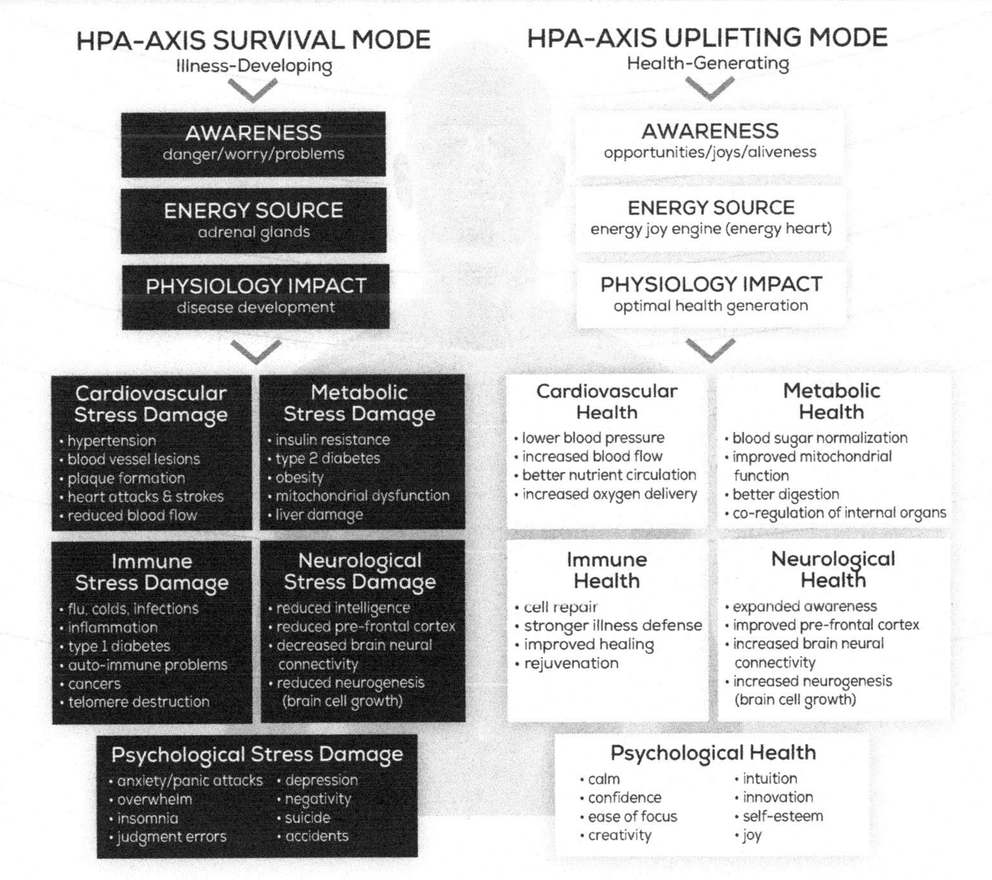

Our biological 'processor' has four main functioning components: a signal, an evaluator, a reaction and thankfully, a tuning component. Tuning is our key to uplift out of survival.

> **Our goal is to re-tune our HPA-axis from only signaling survival issues into signaling opportunities to uplift. Turning on our ENERGY JOY engine completes this four-stage uplifting adventure.**

We humans are now quite skilled at noticing what's wrong. We have become ever-ready to react, fight, become upset, hate, hurt or feel hurt. The problem is that this increasingly results in more stress damage. Living that way is simply not healthy. As we better comprehend how reality works here on Earth, we begin to realize how we are perpetuating — continuously and needlessly — a reality of more and more stress damage.

The body's survival reaction, stuck ON in most people globally, results in 'stressed out' being a near constant state. Most people do not know how to get unstuck, because they do not know how to operate their own biological processor, their HPA-axis.

The consequences are enormous. Although we want to believe that tiny daily stresses are nothing and are normal, the truth is different. Adding an extended pandemic, too many of our population around the world are now in mental health crises.

A deeper look at the common phrase 'stressed out' is revealing.

4

'STRESSED OUT'

Of What?

When you're 'stressed out', what exactly are you stressed out of?

When you are stressed out, you are literally out of health, out of focus needed for being either productive or successful, out of calm, out of fuller awareness and out of enjoying your life.

But even more dangerous is what your body is actually into.

> **'Stressed out' means you are in a disease development spiral.**

Your HPA-axis is stuck 'on' survival. The longer you're stressed out, the worse it gets.

> **Diseases develop when our opportunity awareness signals have been missed and their messages are being ignored.**

This is because each and every symptom, illness and disease are signals. They are valuable communications with the primary purpose of delivering messages to correct something. When we get that message and correct accordingly, the symptom, illness and disease can dissolve.

Getting this message is the secret of 'cause' and 'cure'.

Stress signals increasingly enter our awareness, forcing us to deal with them so that we receive its messages.

Our stress signals arrive in increasingly damaging stages. The goal is to catch them as early as you can.

The initial opportunity awareness signal of stress comes in the form of 'unusual sensations'. These we might briefly notice, but then quickly dismiss because it didn't really hurt or it goes away. Since we've not been taught to value or even consider these sensations as important perceptions and purposeful messages, they march up the disease development cycle to become discomforts, which develop into symptoms, then illness and disease – all to get our attention!

Stopping this dangerous decline depends upon simply recognizing the signal, getting its message and making appropriate changes. Then the stress can stop because it has served its actual purpose: to get your attention and deliver helpful information.

First and foremost, illness is a communication. Strange, yet odd at the same time, 'listening' isn't taught.

For example, when your cellphone rings in your personalized tone, that signals you to pay attention because a message is coming through to you. Whether a text, email, video, tweet or a live phone conversation, the signal is delivering information. Your body also has many levels of signaling, and they all deliver important messages.

Disease develops from the equivalent of not answering your phone when it rings. You are ignoring your biological intelligence — at your own peril.

If the message is really important, the caller will keep calling to get your attention. Let's say the ringing gets louder and louder, first distracting you, then annoying you, irritating you and then causing a migraine headache. Or you get so flustered with higher blood pressure that your heart 'attacks' you. This is how the discomfort of tiny, daily stresses become symptoms, illnesses and diseases — all to get your attention to receive the message and correct course in some way that is beneficial.

How widespread is the damage from simply not picking up the phone and getting the message?

Before the pandemic this single event of stress damage in the body caused 60%-80% of all primary care doctor visits[12] and 50% of sick days at work[13]. USA businesses lost $300 billion from this one thing in 2015 alone[14]. The World Health Organization now calls stress 'the epidemic of the 21st century'. Its damage and costs are accelerating.

Despite its costly prevalence, this one event has not been solved nor effectively addressed for many decades.

We're changing that now. We're going to get the message.

Our Opportunity Awareness Signal

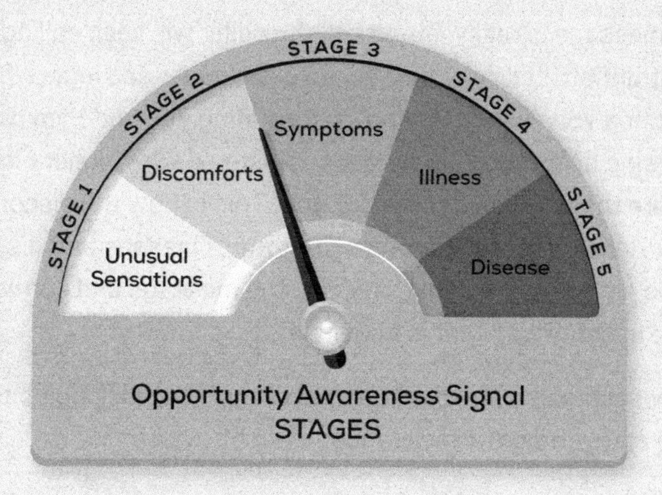

Our Opportunity Awareness Signals are communications with messages to become more aware – in the present – for opportunities to uplift, correct something or enjoy something.

More aware than are we, these signals' mysterious source is the greater intelligence of our creativity, intuition, insight and brilliant solutions. Familiar names for this also include: soul, spirit, higher self and true self.

We grow the relationship with our greater intelligence as genuine self-esteem and self-love by acting upon these Opportunity Awareness Signals at their earliest stages so they don't need to worsen just to get our attention – and so we actually gain the benefits of their guidance – as individuals and as a species.

5

GOT SIGNALS?

Imagine what calamities would ensue at a busy intersection if the red light on a traffic signal didn't turn on at the right time.

Signals are central to health.

The key to operating your HPA-axis effectively is to appreciate the usefulness — and elegance — of understanding stress as your opportunity awareness signal. It is your vehicle for entering the jet stream current of uplifting.

The vital function of cellular signaling, what biologists call 'signal transduction', is to deliver timely information. But instead of tweets and ads, this information is absolutely essential to your body's health.

In Chinese medicine it is said that your glands are the parents to your organs. This means that your organs — heart, lungs, liver, kidney, intestines, pancreas, spleen, gall bladder, etc. — are all continuously directed by the signaling information delivered to them by your glands. The three glands of your HPA-axis help regulate every organ in your body.

But what signals direct them? This is where we're going.

In his authoritative book on the HPA-axis, here is how scientist Dr. Thomas Guilliams describes the importance of signaling for health.

> *"The human body has an amazing ability to maintain its own health when provided with the right amounts and types of healthy signals. When harmful signals are removed and appropriate signals are enhanced, cells and organ systems are capable of creating a healthy outcome.*[15]

> *"While the name we give to chronic diseases might depend on the organ system or tissues involved, such as atherosclerosis, osteoarthritis, Alzheimer's disease, type 2 diabetes, heart disease or cancers,* ***the chronic dysfunction involved in each of these conditions is ultimately caused by the presence of harmful signals that overwhelm tissues' ability to self-heal, or the absence of healthy signals that promote tissue recovery."***[16]

What happens when the information that the signals deliver is simply not received or is distorted?

Diseases such as cancer, auto-immune conditions and endocrine disruptions develop, and can be rightly considered as "diseases of miscommunication".[17,18] The tissues, organs and glands simply do not know what to do to stay healthy. Clueless, they derail from health. They are no longer operating as healthy, functional parts of their greater whole — your body/mind.

Restoring healthy communication offers a key primary goal and very promising direction for both illness prevention AND optimal health. How to nourish healthy signaling can become a special and central discipline for healthcare. We shall soon discover signaling's source of healthy communication.

Decades of experience show that merely 'managing' symptoms does not cure. It can bring temporary relief, but the underlying disease development continues because the messages delivered by these signals are ignored. This is valuable to recognize because the messages reveal both 'cause' and 'cure'.

> **'Cure' has to include restoring healthy signals and correcting unhealthy signals.**

Shifting our focus to cure can elevate healthcare into gaining extraordinary improvements and cost reductions. An optimally healthy population — not a minimally unhealthy one — should be our species' healthcare goal, nationally and globally.

> **Identifying what facilitates optimal signaling and what harms signaling are key to producing an optimally healthy population.**

What blocks healthy signaling?

6

ENEMIES OF LIFE

Healthy cell signaling is blocked, distorted, damaged and eliminated by one major, non-mysterious thing in its many forms: pollution.

The bottom-line resources required for healthy biological life on Earth — for all species — are clean water, fresh (oxygenated) air, living soil microbes, nutritious food and coherent electromagnetic fields. All are now being contaminated — increasingly.

By whom? Who would do such dastardly deeds?

People in polluting industries seem neither informed by common sense nor by basic responsibility to the common good. Damaging these non-negotiable essentials of biological health with products and processes that destroy health as well as damage health signals results in an important global recognition vital for our healthy uplifting.

> **The polluting industries, their investors, owners and management have literally become "enemies of life".**

Pollution is that fundamental and dangerous.

It's like they are in a suicide race, one that takes all of us down with them. They are actively destroying the natural world faster and faster while trying to make and spend as much money as they can before causing extinction — of our species and millions of other species on Earth.

Most of these 'business people' even know the probable final results of their enterprises, but they are more fixated on money than on life. They are actively performing a modern form of Biblically prohibited idolatry.

No matter what chemicals the food industry sneaks into its processed products to trick our taste buds into wanting more, or what nonsense advertisers proclaim, our body can only respond honestly — either with illness or health. We need a 'health o'meter' that can accurately and truthfully determine healthiness free of political and financial corruption.

There is zero mystery about what happens when pollution in its many forms renders healthy signaling pathways dysfunctional. Cells mutate epigenetically in known ways that lead directly to cancers, auto-immune disorders, dementia, diabetes, hypertension, obesity, anxiety and a plethora of disease conditions.[19]

> **From a health signaling perspective, the 5G rush is dangerously foolhardy because it permeates our bodies, our homes and the environment with microwaves that are already known to directly interfere with healthy biological signaling — for all forms of life.**

In 2017, over 230 scientists and physicians around the world signed a letter of appeal to the European Union to halt 5G proliferation until its safety is studied.[20]

Disaster beckons when commercial greed can override health safety.

We need to discover and mandate a more bio-friendly, genuinely nourishing medium for telecommunications. Until we do, valuing health with common sense should legislate that 5G be contained within insulated cables like fiber optics are. This shielding helps prevent both microwave leakage and signal interference. It is also safer, faster, more secure, less costly and more reliable in changing weather conditions.

We need a reality-based capitalism — one that aligns with, nourishes, values and thus financially appreciates healthy biological life as our single greatest asset on Earth. Polluting industries would cease being profitable once they are held financially responsible for repairing their damage, providing clean-up, and for paying to replenish Nature's pre-existing, freely provided 'services' they ruin.[21, 22]

Making money for money's sake, devoid of a value system, is suicidal nonsense when human activities can easily be best motivated by a global economic system that rewards the only real value — nourishing life.

Our species must join biological reality.

What went wrong?

7

WRONG RABBIT HOLE

Signaling and Stress

Why would signaling, which is exquisitely designed for increasing biological health and improving life, create such an expansive array of damaging symptoms, illness and disease development from stress?

As our body's main opportunity awareness signal connects us to reality itself, why are we simply not comprehending its message? Does the signaling of stress have an entirely unknown purpose which we have yet to discover? Could this function be extraordinarily positive, uplifting, vitally important, and expansive — the total opposite to the pervasive destruction of stress damage?

If so, what might its purpose be? And how could it be operating?

When one mechanism single-handedly causes so much damage to health and business, it might be prudent to understand how it does such a fine job of devastation.

Who knows... perhaps healthcare costs can be reduced — greatly. Perhaps people's health can be improved — greatly. Perhaps very easy changes can be implemented nationally to produce an optimally healthy population instead of an increasingly ill one.

And perhaps there is even more wondrous purpose.

To understand this amazing phenomenon, we are going to travel along its sequence of signals. First we go downstream to see how in the world this one mechanism dominates all aspects of health. Then we head upstream to discover the source of its signals.

Revelation shall result.

Stress starts when we perceive something as stressful. This activates our HPA-axis. Our hypothalamus gland releases a hormone called CRF (corticotropin-releasing-factor) that triggers the pituitary gland to release a hormone called ACTH (adreno-cortico-tropic-hormone). This hormone triggers the adrenal glands to release a plethora of hormones.

The most familiar adrenal hormones are cortisol and adrenalin (also called epinephrin and norepinephrine).

This single event, which repeats hundreds of times daily in 'stressed out' people, can keep your HPA-axis constantly activated without rest.

That is the main problem of stress damage.

Why?

Because it causes increasing development of symptoms, illness and disease in a relentless march that deteriorates health and causes rapid aging. Like an accelerating chain reaction, it does so along these five main pathways of stress damage.[23]

- **cardiovascular stress damage** — *hypertension, blood vessel lesions, plaque formation, heart attacks, stroke*

- **metabolic stress damage** — *insulin resistance, type 2 diabetes, obesity, mitochondrial dysfunction, liver damage*
- **immune stress damage** — *flu, colds, infections, inflammation, type 1 diabetes, auto-immune problems, cancers, telomere destruction*
- **neurological stress damage** — *decreased intelligence, reduced pre-frontal cortex (executive) functioning, lowered brain neural connectivity, reduced neurogenesis (new brain cell growth)*
- **psychological stress damage** — *anxiety, overwhelm, insomnia, panic attacks, depression, mistakes, accidents, errors of judgment, negativity, despair, suicide*

Impressive!

While there can be other 'causes' of these problems, the HPA-axis can cause all of these by itself. It too often does. But even when there are other causes, once the HPA-axis gets involved, illness worsens and healing/recovery is then delayed and impeded.

The mechanisms by which these problems are caused can easily fill a medical textbook. And they should. More avenues of stress damage are being discovered daily by researchers around the world.

Solving stress damage will change medicine for the better.

How does stress harm? Here is the 'down and dirty' damage revealed by connecting dots.

Adrenalin

When your adrenal glands release adrenalin, this chemical signal stimulates your heart to beat faster and stronger. Why? Your HPA-axis has judged that you are in a life-or-death survival situation. So it is sending your nutrient rich, oxygen-rich blood to fuel your skeletal muscles so you can physically fight or flee for your life.

Adrenalin is survival level energy.

Brilliant for real dangers, but... today our HPA-axis gets activated from each and every tiny thought that is a worry, problem, frustration, fear, irritation, challenge or merely a change in plans. We need to learn how to steer our mind. This survival reaction keeps your HPA-axis taxed and turned on non-stop, so higher blood pressure can become your new normal.

A serious problem with redirecting blood flow to your skeletal muscles is that this means your internal organs are now receiving a much-reduced blood flow of needed oxygen, nutrients and waste removal. Any organ deprived of optimal blood supply is in trouble. When many organs are deprived for long periods of time, results are disastrous.

Being 'stressed out' causes disease development. Any or all organs can be damaged. This explains the huge variety of stress-induced illnesses.

Without proper blood supply, our digestive organs — stomach, small and large intestines — cannot properly metabolize food into needed nutrients nor eliminate wastes well. Food is undigested.

Let's say adrenalin increases your blood pressure and turbo-charges an undigested food particle in your blood powerfully enough to scratch the inside lining of a blood vessel. That signals white blood cells to quickly gather round to protect and heal that scratch as part of your immune response. They might form a clump. Fat cells traveling in your blood can then stick to that clump and build a plaque formation. The blood vessel pathway narrows, restricting blood flow to whatever organ it supplies. It can even become blocked.

Suppose a bigger stress strikes the tiny village and adrenalin raises your blood pressure enough to knock the plaque formation off its perch atop the scratch. Now you have a fat ball traveling in your blood. If this fat ball lodges to block a blood vessel going to the heart, you get a heart 'attack'. If it lodges to block a blood vessel feeding your brain, you get a stroke. If it blocks a kidney vessel, you can get kidney failure. And so on.

All from tiny, insignificant times of being 'stressed out'.

Cortisol

Your adrenal glands also release cortisol under stress from HPA-axis activation. This hormone can single-handedly cause horrendous havoc, leading to diabetes, obesity, immune weakness and auto-immune disorders.

How?

Cortisol blocks insulin from doing its primary job of signaling cells to open so they can receive glucose for fuel. Cells then become 'insulin resistant'. They start starving. Like a hungry infant, they start screaming for food. They signal us. We get an urge to eat.

Eat what?

We suddenly crave instant energy stuff — like sugar, sweets, fried foods, caffeine and junk food devoid of any nourishment. In an imaginary imperfect world, that should do it.

But... if the cortisol is still stopping insulin from opening the cells, then the glucose remains in our blood. It gets stored as fat. From this one basic stress hormone, type II or 'insulin-resistant' diabetes and obesity can both result. In fact, they do.

And when the fat buildup locates in the belly area, it can herald heart disease, as if we're not supposed to go down that road.

There's more!

During stress, in case we have to wrestle on the ground with a saber-toothed tiger and get scratched, cortisol also signals our thymus gland to release killer T-cells to boost our immune reaction against possible infection. Unfortunately for that brilliant, life-saving reaction, saber-toothed tigers have been extinct for millennia. No more blaming the tigers. Today our worried thinking alone triggers our body's survival reactivity of stress.

If your adrenal glands have tired from being 'stressed out' for too long, and cannot produce enough cortisol, your immune response is weak. This is when colds, flu, susceptibility to virus and infections can take hold, even easing the way for cancer cells to proliferate without being checked.

Killer T-cells are like a weaponized army ready to do battle against an enemy. But with modern mental stress of worries, negativity, despair and depression, there's no physical enemy like infectious microorganisms to fight.

If... your adrenal glands are healthy, they can produce enough cortisol to signal the killer T-cells to stand down and return to their home: your thymus gland. This is the second phase of a healthy immune reaction to stress. Peace is restored.

But, if you have been 'stressed out' for too long, and your adrenal glands are exhausted from constant HPA-axis activations, then they cannot produce enough cortisol to signal the killer T-cells to return home.[24]

What's a self-respecting killer T-cell to do when it's armed and ready to party? Attack!

Attack what? Your own body.

Attacking imaginary enemies like the beta cells in your pancreas that make your body's insulin causes juvenile or type I diabetes. Attacking your nervous system can cause MS or multiple sclerosis. This is how stress damage causes many auto-immune problems.

To add insult to injury, stress reactivity makes us stupid too.

Our brain blood flow leaves the pre-frontal cortex area – our brain's executive C suite – where we make our brilliant decisions with righteous, regal reasoning. Our blood is re-directed to supply our hind brain for survival level instinctual behaviors – pure animalistic fight or flight level thinking that fuels primal anger and fear emotions. Our intelligence, which grows from connecting brain neurons, is blocked. The growth of new brain cells stops.[25]

Could it be that we're not supposed to be 'stressed out' all the time? Did getting stuck in survival send us humans down the wrong rabbit hole?

How do we get out?

To change this entire stress sequence of disease development, we go 'upstream'.

8

THE WIZARD BEHIND THE CURTAIN

Where does a stress reaction actually start? Can stress be headed off at that pass?

How does your body even know it's stressed? Can a more healthy and useful decision be made?

May the answers enthrall you! This means they are filling you with... wonder. These answers SHOULD make you wonder – about many things. This is good because 'wonder' aims your focus into a realm of greater openness. To what?

Awareness. Of what?

When you 'wonder', you are aiming your focus to connect with whatever will bring you the answers you seek. You are basically opening your awareness to tune into something more aware than you. This is the awareness of what wisdom traditions call your 'Big Mind'.

You want to engage your 'Big Mind' because that's where the riches are. We're going there. But I am now just planting a seed into your mind. We are not yet upstream enough for that.

Here's where we are. We now know that the major damage of stress comes from the hormones released by the adrenal glands. But... the adrenal glands do not turn themselves on or off. Like everything in the body, they are signaled.

What tells them to turn on?

Two primary signaling pathways lead to the adrenal glands. One is the HPA-axis route. The adrenals receives the signaling hormone ACTH from the pituitary gland. But the pituitary does not turn itself on either. It receives the signaling hormone CRF from the hypothalamus.

So... the hypothalamus activates the HPA-axis.

Like an electrical jolt, a second signaling pathway brings far faster activation. This comes via our arousal mechanism, the Sympathetic Nervous System (SNS). This super sparks the adrenal glands to release epinephrin and norepinephrine, which instantly incite the heart to pump faster and harder. Again, its purpose is to turbocharge nutrient-rich blood flow from the internal organs outward to fuel the skeletal muscles for a life-or-death survival battle of fighting or fleeing.

> **Yet the Sympathetic Nervous System also does not activate itself. We need to go further upstream.**

Do you know that you have a reptilian brain?

This oldest part of our human brain, around 500 million years old, was the first part of our brain to develop. Called our 'brainstem', it is similar to what more ancient creatures have, such as reptiles. Our brainstem is what operates the pure physiology of our ancient fight or flight survival reaction to give us all the instant energy, focus and mobility we need to survive an intense life-threatening struggle.

A section of this brainstem is called the 'pons'. It has a nucleus called the locus coeruleus. This somehow gives our Sympathetic Nervous System its marching orders.

The locus coeruleus is also what turns on our brain's 'instant alert' that gives us the incredible mental awareness we need in dangerous situations. It does so by triggering norepinephrine (adrenalin) release in the brain, AND it triggers the SNS to activate excitatory responses we feel as stress and panic in the adrenal glands.[26]

Is this it? Is this the source of our stress?

Not yet. The locus coeruleus does not turn itself on either.

> **What triggers the locus coeruleus to signal 'excite' to the brain and the SNS?**

Surprise! This is again our hypothalamus, the 'H' of the HPA-axis. Specifically, it's the lateral part of the hypothalamus, which releases a signaling hormone called orexin that excites the locus coeruleus.

So far, it seems clear that the hypothalamus is 'the black box'. It acts as central command: judge, jury and executioner of all responses that cause stress damage.

But... how does the hypothalamus know what to decide? This seems like a very big job for such a little gland. Is there a tiny homunculus living inside it, frenetically connecting wires like early telephone switchboard operators?

Where does it get its information? What are its decisions based on?

For this, we must continue climbing upstream along the trail of signals until we get to the source.

To be a well-informed decision-maker, the hypothalamus needs to know what's going on — both outside our body in the external world around us and inside our body's internal environment.

The cells that make up the hypothalamus have nuclei that do indeed receive signals — from BOTH our internal environment and our external environment.

Signals come to the hypothalamus with information to update it about our appetite, body temperature, blood sugar, fluid levels and our circadian rhythm — all internal to our body.

These same nuclei also receive signals from our five senses about what's going on in our external environment. Remember, stress is actually an 'opportunity awareness signal'. So it must have access to important information.

The hypothalamus must integrate three main realms of incoming data. This data streams in from several parts of our brain.

First are our emotions. A part of our brain called the amygdala has the ability to interpret emotional signals and 'decide' how we know to have fear. Survival takes priority. This amygdala also keeps memories of what we've been afraid of so it can speed up reactions.

Second is memory-making. A part of our brain called the hippocampus helps form new memories from our experiences and also can make emotional interpretations of these events — like how we feel. The goal is to learn from our experiences so we don't have to repeat the mistakes.[27]

Third is the part of our brain considered the chief executive, where decision-making, planning, problem-solving and social interaction form. This is the prefrontal cortex.

All this goes into the hypothalamus. There are other important questions.

Is the information going into the hypothalamus raw data? Or has it been pre-digested? Is it completely objective? Or... has it already been tampered with, color coded and distorted?

If so, by what?

We still have not arrived at the source of the entire chain of signals that generate stress damage. 'Going upstream' helps explain why decades of treating stress far downstream at the chemical/molecular level has not been effective. That intervention only 'manages' the tail end of this fascinating series of chain reactions.

'Going upstream' has promise. It might just solve stress.

9

WHAT RULES YOUR MIND

Going even further upstream, all the judgments of our hypothalamus — from both our external environment and our internal milieu — come from an even higher, more inclusive level of neurological organization. All that we perceive — everything from our five senses, from our chief executive's reasonings in the prefrontal cortex and from all the emotional interpretations of our amygdala and hippocampus — are in service of fulfilling something non-physical.[28]

Something non-physical, non-chemical and non-molecular directs our reactions to just about everything in our life. It is what chooses between right and wrong, good and bad, true and false.

What is this?

Our core values.

> **'Values' operate as the frontline filter of our perception.**

Values give us our personal reality by selectively prioritizing, changing, reacting to and/or ignoring information. Our values direct, choose, decide, command and determine our very awareness of reality.

What we see, hear, taste, smell and feel are first influenced by our values — before we become conscious of their content. Our values are the cause of our subjectivity, judgments, priorities, likes and dislikes.

In short, our values dictate and control our reactions to stress.

Yet most people are not conscious of their own values. Or that their values are in a hierarchy, with some more valuable than others.

> **Your most important value rules you.**

Do you know yours?

Are values the wizard behind the curtain? Or are they just the curtain?

Are we done? We have traveled far up the rabbit hole. But have we caught the rabbit?

PART II:

PHYSICAL MEETS ENERGY

Understanding how biological energy
works best – for us and for Life –
is now necessary for our
continued survival.

10

HOW DO VALUES WORK?

We have a couple of big problems with our values.

Their unbridled power has somehow made humans dangerous to all life on Earth.

Like letting the genie out of its bottle, we have become unwitting pawns, victims and servants of fearsome forces we ourselves have unleashed but don't comprehend.

To fix them we need to understand what values really are, and how they operate to determine our entire conscious reality – especially the calamitous damage of stress. Then we'll need to choose.

Values are like the seeds of plants. They grow non–physical fruit. By being the guardian and gatekeeper to what is right/wrong, true/false and good/bad, their fruit continually blossoms as our wants, needs and desires.

Our values control us, motivate us and direct us.

Like sprouting roots that spread into the fertile soil of our mind, **our values also grow our beliefs.**

Beliefs are interesting in their influence, because if we believe something is true, right or good, then it is indeed so — for us. And if we believe something is false, bad or wrong, then it is indeed so — for us.

In this way our beliefs give our reality both fluidity and inflexibility.

But changing our beliefs or anyone else's beliefs is really challenging.

This is because beliefs filter the information that comes to us to match them. All information is filtered — both from our external environment through our five senses and internally through our thoughts. Like a cell's semi-permeable membrane, some things are welcomed in and some are blocked out.

Except... what gets in or pushed out literally determines our personal reality — our awareness. And it affects others we interact with.

Our beliefs spread like branches of a mental tree, usually in a garden of related beliefs like a mental ecosystem. These branches in turn sprout leaves and flowers as our operating principles and teachings that guide something hugely important.

> **Your values dictate how you steer your focus to direct your energy.**

Like a self-fulfilling feedback loop, whatever information or experiences you have — including everything your receive from your five senses — you feed as fertilizer/vitamins back into validating, proving and sustaining your beliefs that emerge from your values. This is having the 'mind like a steel trap'.

> **Your values also tell you how to use your time.**

Like living in a Star Trek 'holodeck' that creates your thoughts into virtual reality, this is how you propagate your actual reality.

Our entire species is also doing this self-fulfilling reality propagation, and quite unconsciously. Self-fulfillment can help us navigate life more easily, if... accurately based in reality. Accurate reality feedback is why we need the signaling of stress.

> **Stress results as an awareness signal to deliver the opportunity to align better with reality — when our expectations, wants and needs are in conflict with reality.**
>
> ***Expectation versus Reality = Stress***

For example, if you value health highly, then you want to be more healthy. This naturally leads you to discover more about health, to search for what makes health and avoid what destroys health. If you have suffered an illness that Western medicine couldn't fix, which most people have, then you likely have begun to explore traditional plant remedies, herbs, vitamins, acupuncture, chiropractic, homeopathy, energy modalities and other naturopathic therapies. You might come across a fact of science and give its recommendation a try. If it works, you might then include certain sciences as resources for you to enjoy health.

Soon, you grow a set of beliefs about science and about health. Armed with these beliefs, your quest is streamlined so you don't have to think anew about everything. You just add new leaves of information.

Your beliefs are now guiding your thoughts and actions about health — your value.

From here, as a social creature, you might want to project your value of health onto other people too. You might become motivated to become an herbalist, biodynamic farmer or chiropractor.

Or you might discover that your personal health greatly depends on having access to healthy food and clean water, fresh air, living soil microbes, a healthy environment, a healthy civilization and a healthy planet.

Now an entire pantheon of morals, ethics, integrity, philosophy, social action, politics, scientific truths and philanthropic causes can grow and connect like a neural network of fungi underneath the soil — complete with allies and opponents, friends and foes. Naturally you seek out, congregate with and attract people who share your highest value.

In a sense, you are radiating your values and their fruit out into the world. It's not physical, but it impacts the physical world through your actions, speech, thoughts and intentions.

> **You are directing your energy to affect reality with your sustained focus.**

We utilize energy to create our values into being. We are painting a picture into physical reality, like a virus spreads throughout a body.

The question becomes... is it a good virus or a harmful one?

Let's say your highest value is making money. This value creates your beliefs, your principles, your ethics and motivates your actions.

You begin a quest to learn how to become wealthy. You digest such concepts as present value, opportunity costs and multiple income streams. You discover that the fastest, biggest money-making vehicle in the world is weapons manufacturing. Bombs have a huge profit margin. As long as there are wars, ammunition needs constant re-ordering. You discover that you can sell to parties on all sides of any conflict. Markets can be expanded simply by promoting conflicts, uprisings and wars. So you hire media experts to generate hatred and distrust with lies, deceitful slogans and violent images that create distrust and enemies.

Profits exponentially expand as you discover how destruction is a fundamentally necessary tool for later getting construction contracts with new partners to rebuild the infrastructure your products have demolished. You can also scoop up the natural resources of war's victims for cheap, and hire now desperate laborers for cheap. It's a massive profit-accelerator.

Naturally you seek out, congregate with and attract people who share your highest values: money and power. International opportunities abound. You can sell your weapons and the entire package deal to anyone with similar ambition for money or power. Or you just jump into a potential market uninvited. Your highest value of making money deems it beautiful and brilliant.

As a highest value, you are directing your energy to affect reality. You are utilizing energy to create your values into being. Like a spreading virus, you blossom its fruit out into the world as an entire pantheon of morals, ethics, integrity, philosophy, social action, politics, scientific truths and causes.

Is it a good virus or a harmful one?

Perhaps in your quest to make money as your highest, most prized value, you choose to enter the resource extraction business of mining. Coal, fossil fuels and natural gas seem like obvious money-makers. Now you grow beliefs from your value that help you focus your energy. In this case as well, your beliefs filter out anything conflicting with your value — like contaminating waterways with your waste products, polluting the air every living thing breathes or killing the soil's living microbes that make food nutrient-rich and healthy. All this is secondary if not nonsensical compared to the primacy of your value — making money. You seek out, congregate with and easily attract people in government who share your value of money and happily use their position to do so — for money. Everyone agrees to collaborate in creating a money-making project. You might even join with weapon-makers to keep protesting people from stopping your money flow.

It can become a closed system where your reality is dictated by your values, and your values are reinforced by your reality.

But... what if you want the big three — more money, more power and more control — but without wars and obvious conflict? You choose to enter the pharmaceutical industry, where you can capture a large market by patenting an essential medication for an illness that millions of people suffer from. Your big medication doesn't even have to work, if you can just advertise it repeatedly and convince doctors to prescribe it with data manipulated by a swarm of scientists-for-hire. All you need is liability protection from any adverse injuries that it causes in people — easy to do with money for the politicians and regulators who share your love of money.

But because there is no concept of 'enough' when it comes to craving the combination of money, power and control, you naturally want to expand. Now all you have to do is figure out how to 'convince' more and more people to buy your pharmaceutical products.

Your natural allies are people who also value more money, power and/or control. You might consider hiring a laboratory of hungry scientists to create a really super-contagious virus that spreads like wildfire around the world AND can only be contained by your vaccine. To succeed, you just have to hire marketers, journalists and government spokespeople to dramatically build fear of the virus, and claim a tax-deductible business expense, the promotional necessity for selling your vaccine.

By enticing media, world leaders and heads of institutions around the globe — those who share your quest for money, power and control — to participate in your ruse, you orchestrate a global pandemic. Any physicians, scientists, virologists, investigative journalists and epidemiologists who dare present facts and genuine science to dispute the credibility of your venture and attempt to reveal your scam get censored — because you have also partnered with the handful of owners of mass media.

Because there's still no such thing as 'enough', you finesse forcing people to have to take your product that somehow only works for a short time period, so repeating purchases become the norm, like keeping up with the latest fashions. Once established, your entire enterprise can keep cranking out new lab-created illnesses and their treatments — all patented by you but sharing royalties with your many partners.

Of course you want to keep track of everybody to insure your control, so you team up with makers of high tech surveillance devices. They promise that 5G can be calibrated to emit precise frequencies that activate the specific ingredients in your vaccine to make people do all kinds of things you wish, from sprouting new illnesses to dying.

So you put a variety of substances into the vaccines as an experiment to test which ingredients increase things like passivity, immune failure, heart attacks, dementia, cancer and death — just in case you decide there are far too many people populating the Earth when you want more of it for yourself and your buddies.

If you are really clever and have the resources, you can control nearly everything and everyone by being a central banker. Then you just print money whenever you want – for free – and make zillions by charging interest for its use. Banks, corporations, countries and people all pay you interest because the entire financial system is based on debt. Even though the printed money is no longer backed by anything of value, people have to accept it as payment because it's use is enforced as 'legal tender'. Your biggest interest charges are gained from printing money to fund all sides of wars, because country leaders are then most desperate for access to money so they can purchase more weapons. If a country defaults on the loan, just print more money for free and increase the loan so they can at least keep paying you interest. Get Congress to make all big bank loans guaranteed unknowingly by the taxpayers, so risky lending is not an issue – to you. The only challenge is to keep people believing that the central bank is part of our government and not privately owned. Just putting a word like 'federal' into its name does the trick. Adding the word 'reserve' might make people imagine that the printed money is actually backed by something of value.*

It starts with expressing our values.

So... what exactly are values?

> **The best way — perhaps the only true way — to understand how values work is to move into an energy-based understanding of reality.**

From this point onward, you may wish to buckle your mental seatbelt, because I'm taking your mind on a ride — ultimately, a joy ride.

We are now going further upstream.

---

* A fascinating glimpse into the world of central banking can be found in G. Edward Griffin's book: *The Creature from Jekyll Island – A Second Look at the Federal Reserve.*

11

THE ENERGY OF VALUES

We now know that everything physical is made of energy. Any type of matter can theoretically be disassembled into chemicals, then into its increasingly smaller molecules, atoms and sub-atomic ingredients — like electrons, protons and neutrons. Physics, medicine and science in general have been about 'going small'.

Although it's a two-way interaction, what can be overlooked is that the small is directed by the large.

> **Values are also made of energy. Like tuning your radio, values function as a sort of energy channel that receives energy, transforms that energy and then broadcasts out the newly transformed energy to match itself.**

But values do not create energy by themselves. They only direct energy.

Like pouring dough into a cookie mold, values are a pattern through which the energy they receive is molded and exported. As an energy pattern, values influence our perception, thinking, emotions, speech, relationships and behaviors. Our life and our reality are completely colored by the impacts from the energy pattern we call our values.

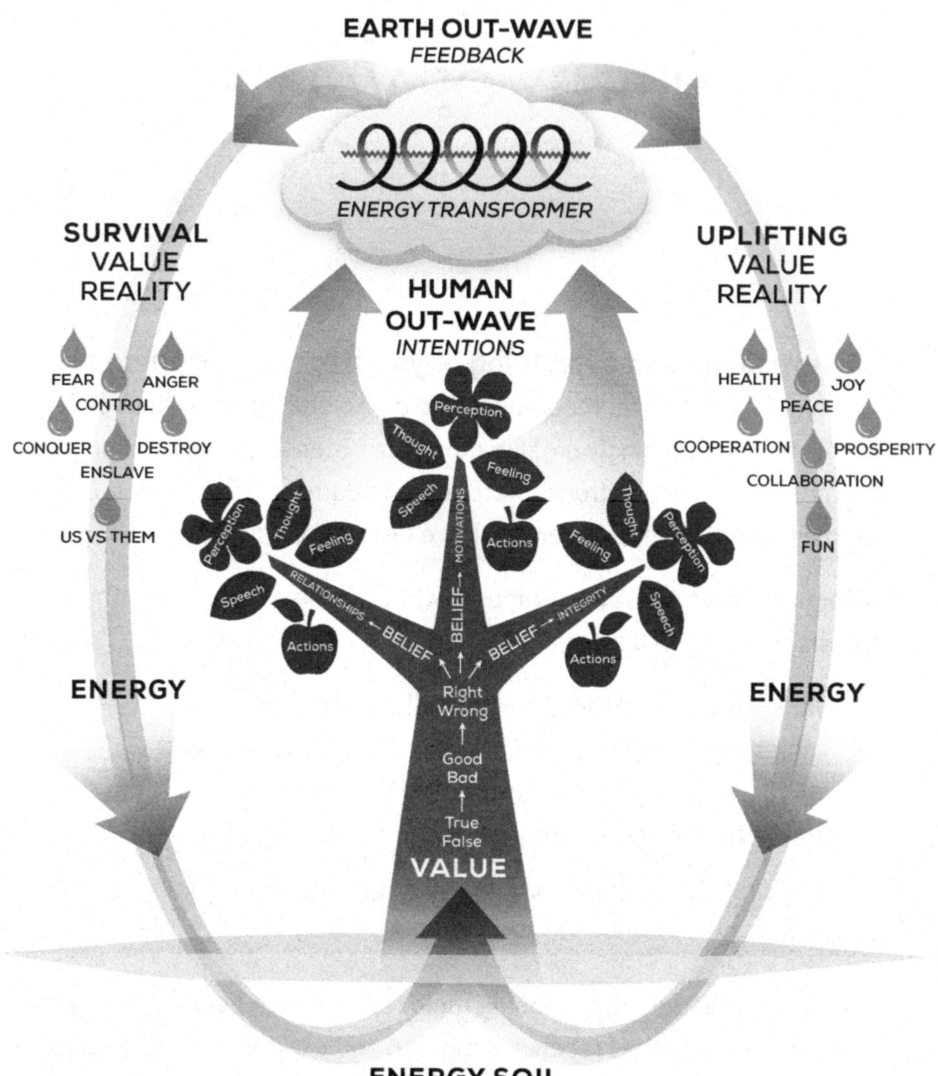
EARTH'S ENERGY ECO-SYSTEM
EARTH OUT-WAVE
FEEDBACK
ENERGY TRANSFORMER
SURVIVAL
VALUE
REALITY
FEAR
ANGER
CONTROL
CONQUER
DESTROY
ENSLAVE
US VS THEM
UPLIFTING
VALUE
REALITY
HEALTH
JOY
PEACE
COOPERATION
PROSPERITY
COLLABORATION
FUN
HUMAN
OUT-WAVE
INTENTIONS
Perception
Thought
Feeling
Speech
Actions
MOTIVATIONS
RELATIONSHIPS
INTEGRITY
BELIEF
Right
Wrong
Good
Bad
True
False
VALUE
ENERGY
ENERGY
ENERGY SOIL

Earth's Energy Eco-System

How our values transform energy into our reality

Water evaporates up into the atmosphere from our lakes, oceans and rivers to form moisture-filled clouds that cycle water back as rain and snow to nourish life on Earth. Likewise, the combined energy that our human species emits from our dominant value interacts with the energy 'atmosphere' of our biosphere as a creative dialogue.

Our top value rules our focus, which directs energy in ways that govern our lives and produce our energy 'out-waves' that communicate our intentions – as individuals and as a species – to the living, conscious energy matrix of our Earth Mother's being. She then grows these energy seeds as part of her energy out-waves that become our physical reality. This fundamental "energy-into-reality" feedback mechanism is Nature's patient guidance to teach us how to grow a better reality.

Our further evolution depends on our choosing to uplift humanity out of mere survival by cultivating the two most functional values all species share because they positively nourish the biological reality of Earth life: health and joy. Our species' grand contribution to the biosphere, increasingly essential to secure our survival, is to harness this for good.

While our Earth Mother grows things and grows thoughts into things, OUR values grow OUR thoughts into things. Our values focus us at THE most influential level possible. They govern our lives.

> **Our values direct our energy to create the stuff of our life – according to them.**

The pattern of a value can be learned as a child and then passed along in families for generations, with each successive generation teaching it and adding fertilizing thoughts as energy that strengthen its pattern. Cultures and religions also teach us our values.

Pouring energy into that pattern we call a value – especially by living, behaving and organizing our lives around that value – makes it quite a substantial force or power. Having a value that you are not living by creates guilt and robs self-esteem.

Our values help us to run our lives on autopilot. We rarely question our values, which can remain invisible to us, until... we bump into a dilemma that involves a clash of values. Then we have to stop and decide which value is more important. This is the essence of a 'mid-life crisis'.

For example, once you learn how to drive a car, you are free to simply steer it to wherever you want to go. You don't have to keep thinking of every nuance of driving, as it's become automatic. But... occasionally another car might run into us, or road conditions cause us to crash. Like driving, to prevent crashes in values, we learn to steer with greater awareness.

> **Values form the most powerful focusing pattern we have.**
>
> **Upgrading our values is called 'growth'. We can choose our values to uplift.**

Which values do we want to guide us as a species?

Our human species is at such a decision point.

12

HUMAN VALUES DISEASE

Unique to humans, we have created a new disease — an energy disease.

Just as opportunistic bacteria can infect your body, this human energy disease infects reality itself.

We have VD — values disease.

Because of our current values, we are violating the single most fundamental biological law on Earth. This is a real law, not a man-made governing principle, not a social contract, nor even a religious doctrine.

Violating this law results in a final sentence that is non-negotiable, inescapable and unavoidable. The consequences are inevitable — a direct cause and effect.

There are no 'second chances', no attorneys to argue our case, no judges to bribe nor political appointees to intervene on our behalf. No military might can change the outcome.

The sentence could be the extinction of our entire species. The end of human civilization on Earth as we know it — and possibly no more humans.

The values that are currently directing human activities are destroying all the biological sources needed for life. These are diseased values.

Even though our human species has been around for many hundreds of thousands of years, we have yet to evolve a species-wide value more ambitious than basic survival. Given the enormous impact of our values on every aspect of our lives, and on the health of the planet, it is time that we recognize the need to uplift out of our current quagmire — BEFORE our focus, locked onto survival, accelerates into a non-stoppable death spiral.

It is time to stop and decide which value is THE most important for humanity.

This has to be a species-wide decision — one that brings our entire human species into agreement. No exceptions. Every human must be able to rely upon this — completely.

And it must be the highest value. It must activate a most important function.

What would that be?

13

THE REAL SURVIVAL OF THE FITTEST

Like Star Trek's mission, biological life on Earth has its 'prime directive'.

This is to NOURISH LIFE.

Nourishing life is our only true ticket to enjoying life on Earth. Everybody wins — because everyone is nourishing life. Somehow, our species must choose this winning value, agree to honor it AND implement it in all our endeavors. Why would we not?

We humans can then enter a much larger, more fun playground.

> **All species play. It's the joy of life. They have fun.**

All other species on Earth nourish life — every single one — except for humans. The deal is that every species adds value to life — every species. Or they lose the right to survival. Every species' survival must be earned. How?

By making contributions so immense and essential, each species establishes itself as highly valuable to the other species in our biosphere.

THIS is the real 'survival of the fittest'.

Survival of the 'fittest' means fit to do what? GIVE. It alone earns the rewards of being beneficial to the entire biosphere. The community of living beings vote you IN. They love you. They help you with their nourishing contributions. This is the only true membership card into the club of biological life.

We and every species on Earth are here to contribute to life – to be a healthy, functioning – ie contributing – part of the greater whole that is the entire biosphere.

> *"Nothing in Nature lives for itself. Rivers don't drink their own water. Trees don't eat their own fruit. The Sun doesn't shine for itself. Flowers don't spread fragrance for themselves. Living for others is the rule of Nature." (anonymous)*

This is 'The Law' and the only true ticket to continuing human life. It is the most basic of biological intelligence. We humans are here to provide such value to the entire biosphere, that all the other species love us, and want us to be part of the community of living beings. They choose to help us do what we're contributing because it nourishes them.

With us they can enjoy life better.

Adding value to life is the real competition amongst all species. We are all here to give something most precious, uplifting, strengthening, joyous and healthy – things beautiful to life. It's a competition that only creates winners.

Biological life in our Earth Mother is supposed to be a celebration.

It will be a most magnificent party as soon as we humans turn all our attention, all our resources, all our innovations and all our activities to enriching life.

This is the "Big Win".

Imagine... all human activities, all organizations, all governments, all institutions and all peoples dedicated to adding value to life as their primary purpose. Actually, we must do more than merely imagine. We must implement.

But how do we know what to contribute?

Our biological intelligence delivers this knowledge in the form of our 'opportunity awareness signals'. But modern humans, except for indigenous peoples, seem devoid of this essential key to our survival.

> **"Nature appears to maximize mutual cooperation and mutual coordination of goals. To be indispensable to the organisms with which one shares an environment — that is the strategy that ensures successful breeding and continued survival. It is a strategy in which communication and sensitivity to signal processing are paramount. These are language skills."**[29]

At some point in our pre-history, one of the first biological organisms, the eukaryotes, figured out how to save considerable time and effort — energy — needed to locate food. Instead of spending their entire daily existence hunting food to merely survive, an aberrant eukaryote decided to simply eat another biological organism which had done that work and imbibed it as energy food.[30]

It was brilliant. Lazy, but brilliant.

> **This is likely where the entire 'survival' instinct originated, along with its derivative human personality traits like narcissism, greed and selfishness.**

It is speculated that in some cases, the gene pool increased by trial and error of ingesting other organisms which had developed their own DNA. Over time, some organisms were deemed as good food, while others were incorporated as 'partners' that join together to share DNA — resulting in a gain of biological intelligence.

Single-celled organisms became multi-celled organisms. In time, the cooperation led to specialization of contribution, where some early organisms agreed to become the eyes and sense organs of the host organism, while others became the best arms to grab and best teeth to chew prey. All of our current organs, glands, muscles, tissues, bones and nerve cells have likely developed from this journey of contributing to 'the greater whole'.

As a fascinating example of mutual cooperation by creating value, we can applaud the mitochondria, the energy production factories in all our cells. All of our activities — eating, breathing, digesting, metabolizing as well as much of the efforts we make to grow food, afford food etc. — are all to serve our mitochondria. We are serving them. We feed them what they want.

Why?

Because in return, they convert what we eat and breathe into the energy that fuels our existence. We can run, work, move, think and build things because of the biological energy that our mitochondria give us. It's quite a lovely partnership. Indispensable.

But what are our mitochondria?

They are not exactly 'us'. They have their own DNA apart from ours. Yet we both win by cooperating.

How do we know what to give that nourishes life?

To know what adds value, we tune ourselves in a special way — an ancient way — to receive the right information. We have to open to a special flow.

A metaphor for this guidance is in the Biblical story of the Israelites' 40 years in the desert. They knew when to set up camp and when to travel by the 'cloud' above the makeshift temple-on-wheels. This cloud was considered the presence of the Creator. When it settled over the temple, they made camp. When it lifted, they traveled and followed it.

The desert symbolizes difficulty, hardship and the struggles of life. We learn from these. Like the cloud, we have guidance and we have a source to access our guidance.

Our biological processor, our HPA-axis, directs and informs us. When operating properly, it becomes our tuning device to do this quite well. In fact, this is the actual function of stress as our 'opportunity awareness signal'. Stress is not a random, meaningless irritation. It is a fantastically amazing communication apparatus that connects our awareness to the source of its messaging that is far more aware than we are.

Activating our biological intelligence is what opens and maintains our access to this source. What exactly is this source?

Upstream we go!

14

YOUR ENERGY SKIN

Keeping in mind that stress is an 'awareness signal', one way to understand this is by going further upstream toward the apex of biological signaling's hierarchy.

Recent research in quantum biology points to all of our bodily functions being directed by signaling from something that surrounds and permeates our body like an 'energy skin'.

This is our body's electromagnetic field.[31]

This energy skin is increasingly understood as the higher level of organization that instructs our brain. It is the 'greater whole' from which comes the more coherent signaling that is continually telling all our glands, organs, tissues and cells what to do.[32]

At its higher level of organization, the field reigns. The field embodies what we call our 'mind'. Our mind controls our physical brain. Having a healthy, optimally functioning energy field to direct coherent signaling is paramount. This electromagnetic field is itself connected to and constantly communicating with the larger fields of our immediate surroundings, the environment, our Earth Mother's living energy matrix and beyond.

Somewhere within our energy field is the likely location of the filter for our awareness we call our values.

This makes sense when we consider how we perceive through our five physical senses.

Our eyes 'see' visible light. Actually, instead of bestowing us with sight, they serve mainly to restrict and limit our vision so we do NOT see x-ray, ultraviolet, infrared and other parts of the fuller spectrum of light. Our ears are similarly designed to 'hear' only a narrow range of frequencies, not the higher range that bats and dogs perceive, nor the lower range that whales and elephants can hear.

Why such restrictions?

These limitations help stabilize our awareness within the bounds of the physical plane of biological life — for survival.

But what we are really perceiving, whether as visible light frequencies or as vibrations of sound, is energy.

The energy has information encoded within it, and the energy delivers that information to our senses, which further filter and deliver it to our brain — where we can 'make sense' of the energy — based on our values and their associated beliefs.

A growing number of people around the world today can directly perceive this energy field with their eyes. Not just around humans, energy fields are around plants, animals, birds and more — available to those who can see. It's incredibly beautiful, like 'auras'.

How do we gain this fascinating ability to see energy fields?

Wisdom traditions for millennia have secretly trained their prized students to do just this. Once humans manage to survive on our physical planet, we are supposed to move up into these more interesting awarenesses.

We are not supposed to get stuck in mere survival.

The electromagnetic field, our energy skin, is a more aware part of us. It is first to perceive everything from our environment before filtering and delivering its information to our five senses. Our energy field is actually both our first line of illness defense and our first line of perception.

Although our energy field is not our 'soul', the science of it helps us to better fathom how things work in reality.

We live in a sea of energy that comes to us in layers of successively greater wholes. Science has specialized in drilling down into the tiniest details of one of these layers, the chemical molecular and the quantum.

However, going further upstream provides the dots of reality we now need to connect.

We seek to know... how do we best operate our energy field 'mind'?

PART III:

TUNING TO UPLIFT

Uplifting is our species'

most important next step.

We just need to turn on dormant

elements in our physiology.

15

TUNING YOUR BODY / MIND TO UPLIFT

It should be no surprise to realize that throughout human history every culture has examples of extraordinary individuals called sages, wise people, prophets and phenomenal healers. These people were reported to have been able to 'know' things unseen, accurately predict future events, transform material objects with their mind, and even understand the languages of plants, animals, birds, fish and insects.

They could accurately 'read' the information that energy delivers free of normal human filters.

Their abilities and knowledge developed from 'tuning' their body/mind/energy in specific ways that ancient wisdom traditions have refined over millennia. Science can now begin to describe the main components of this tuning, which is indeed the guiding mechanism for evolving our species.

Interestingly, it also fixes our stress. This is because...

> **The HPA-axis is our tuner. The extensive damage stress causes IS our awareness signal to tune our HPA-axis up.**

Like checkmate forces one player to concede losing a game of chess, we now have to tune our HPA-axis up, if only to prevent disease development from stress damage. Then we'll be able to discover its real benefits.

How do we best tune our HPA-axis?

We start with our 'body/mind'.

While science separates our body's parts into individual organs, glands, tissues, cells and molecules, the body itself is a larger whole, a complete system that includes the mind. In truth, everything in the body is connected. Our healthcare system has focused on repairing parts, but not on fortifying the whole.

We can feel much better with less effort by operating at the level of our greater whole, because this gives us greater control over its many parts and makes them optimally healthy.

When it comes to stress, only four body systems are responsible for causing virtually all stress symptoms. If unchecked, these become illnesses and diseases. They do this when they are derailed from health and stuck in the disease development mode called 'stressed out'.

Swiftly restoring healthy HPA-axis functioning, the key ingredient for success, requires simply putting these four major body systems back into their proper operation. Fortunately, directing them back into health is easy and quick — doable within six seconds flat. Then no symptoms, illness and diseases of stress have opportunities to develop.

This means up to 80% of primary care doctor visits and 50% of sick days at work, and their costs, can be easily prevented with a handful of skills — not pills — that reset these four body systems from stress to health.

What parts operate together as our HPA-axis' greater whole?

The functional components for HPA-axis health are :

1. sympathetic nervous system (SMS)
2. parasympathetic nervous system (PSNS)
3. central nervous system (CNS)
4. skeletal muscle system (SMS)

As a reward for choosing health, each body system delivers a 'health treasure' when its optimal function is restored.

Each body system has a corresponding 'Treasure Mode' that produces optimal health instead of its 'Disease Development Mode' when being stressed out. The goal is to quickly recognize when any of these body systems has derailed from health into stressed out, and swiftly restore their functioning into their Treasure Mode.

Decades of stress management techniques have usually left out one or more of these four major systems. Any outlying system can keep re-triggering the HPA-axis so there's no lasting relief — just constant attempts to reduce stress. This 'after-the-fact' damage control is not proactive enough to constitute a cure.

You want to be the Sherlock Holmes of your body, because:

When you realize that every discomfort and symptom of stress, including anxiety itself, is an 'opportunity awareness signal', you enter a living detective game!

As your curiosity grows, you can identify the actual opportunity being presented to you — from a benevolent source more aware than you. Knowing your personal stress signs as your early warning signals gives you great advantage, because you can utilize this unique form of intuition speaking through your body.

Once you become aware of your personal signals, you want to tune in and receive its message of opportunity. Like answering a ringing phone stops its ringing so you can hear the conversation, instantly de-activating your HPA-axis from increasing stress damage is THE skill to have.

Getting that message dissolves the stress because it has then served its only purpose, to communicate the opportunity to you. This is true of all symptoms, illnesses and diseases. They are communications to correct course in some way.

With the health skill called 'Dynamic Calm', all four systems can be flipped from disease development (stressed out) into their corresponding health treasures in seconds.

Let's learn how with these easy-to-learn health skills. To enjoy their maximal benefits and gain their health treasures, you'll want to practice so you can apply them in any life situation with ease.

The first skill is to know your personal 'opportunity awareness signals'. Here is a chart to check each and every type of signals you experience. Once completed, go back and circle the first three signals you usually are aware of. This is like answering the phone on the very first ring. As you develop greater awareness, your stress phone won't need to ring at all. You head stress off at that pass.

You'll just know.

Take Your Stress Damage Test

Check Your Opportunity Awareness Signals From the List Below

STEP 1. Check all your signals below that you notice when you're getting stressed.
STEP 2. Then circle three signals you notice first. Knowing your early warnings for "opportunity awareness" grows your intuition for sensing change and tells you WHEN to pro-actively prevent stress damage before any can occur with Dynamic Calm skills.

SKELETAL MUSCLE SYSTEM | tensed, cramped and tight muscles

[ ] tension headaches
[ ] stomach knots
[ ] neck/throat tension
[ ] forehead pressure
[ ] jaw clenching
[ ] clenched fists
[ ] chest tightness
[ ] temple tension
[ ] teeth grinding
[ ] shoulder tightness
[ ] lower back pain
[ ] shaky hands

AUTONOMIC NERVOUS SYSTEM | emotions, internal organs, hormones & glands

[ ] easily upset
[ ] high blood pressure
[ ] anxious/nervous
[ ] cold hands or feet
[ ] feeling hopeless, helpless
[ ] constipation or diarrhea
[ ] feeling overwhelmed
[ ] afraid for no reason
[ ] depression
[ ] unhappy for no reason
[ ] rapid, shallow breath
[ ] dizzy/lightheaded
[ ] racing heartbeat
[ ] feeling rejected
[ ] frequent frustration
[ ] upset stomach
[ ] clammy hands
[ ] rashes, allergies
[ ] anger & irritation
[ ] migraines
[ ] fatique

CENTRAL NERVOUS SYSTEM | mental activity changes

[ ] racing thoughts
[ ] constant worrying
[ ] dwelling on problems
[ ] easily distracted
[ ] poor concentration
[ ] panic, overwhelm
[ ] negativity
[ ] thinking of future & past
[ ] insomnia
[ ] impatience
[ ] forgetful
[ ] speech problems

BEHAVIORAL STRESS | changes in daily performance, activities, conduct & manners

[ ] arguing with people
[ ] withdrawing from friends
[ ] disconnecting from others
[ ] avoiding tasks & duties
[ ] increasing alcohol/drugs
[ ] daydreaming more often
[ ] snappping at people
[ ] crying easily
[ ] appetite gain or loss

More than three unresolved signals indicate you can:

1. Benefit greatly and prevent further illness development
2. Easily remedy these stress related symptoms with THE STRESS FIX skills
3. Gain remarkable health benefits as you apply the vital messages stress delivers

Doing nothing is a health gamble because unresolved symptoms can quickly develop into serious illness and immune problems. Costs then increase exponentially – and unnecessarily. Now you can better prevent a lifetime of stress damage to your health, performance and quality of life.

16

EMOTIONAL CALM

Uplifting Treasure #1

Sympathetic Nervous System

Your sympathetic nervous system gives you the amazing health treasure of relief just by flipping it out of the stress reactivity that triggers adrenalin, raises blood pressure, increases heart rate and moves blood flow from organs to skeletal muscles — while generating the survival emotions of anger and fear with the physiological sensations of anxiety and panic.

What is it worth to you to feel soothing calm whenever you want?

Knowing how to quiet emotional turmoil with genuine serenity — no matter what's going on in your life around you — bestows a deep level of confidence, trust in your body and authentic self-esteem. You feel good.

You feel like YOU!

Enjoying emotional calm also functions as a gateway into all the positive emotions like joy, love, happiness, contentment and feeling safe. You are always one small step closer to enjoying your life.

Yet its energetic tuning functions are even more profound. Emotional calm makes it much easier to focus fully enough to perceive the subtle energies and their messages of guidance, intuition and creativity. It's very hard to tune into that more refined awareness with survival emotions and stress physiology dominating your focus.

Like taking your foot off the gas pedal of stress, a simple, three-step breathing maneuver immediately turns off SNS arousal, lowers blood pressure and relaxes the blood vessel walls so blood flow returns from muscles to nourish your internal organs.

Most important is step #3, resting after the exhale. This is when your body signals your brain that everything is so safe and comfortable that you are not even in a rush to take your next breath of air.

It doesn't get more relaxed than that!

Resting after the exhale is the opposite of how we breathe in a life-threatening fight or flight survival situation. In times of danger we tend to hold our breath after inhaling quickly. This 'breath-holding' is THE breathing pattern of stress, anxiety and panic. It can and does mechanically trigger panic attacks all by itself.

Holding the breath literally raises blood pressure via what is called the 'thoracic pump'. More damage comes from not exhaling the carbon dioxide, because it then forms carbonic acid in the blood which makes the blood pH more acidic. This in turn can cause blood vessels going to the brain to narrow — to protect the brain's delicate environment from the excess carbon dioxide. Dizziness, light-headedness, confusion and even fainting can result. Often hyperventilation then gets triggered to restore pH balance by blowing out the extra CO_2.

The moral: Don't hold your breath. Check your breathing during the day, especially if you're feeling stressed or anxious. Replace breath-holding with the Deep Sigh Breath and feel better immediately!

To see for yourself how effective this is, please take your pulse and/or your blood pressure before trying the Deep Sigh Breath. Do six or eight of these breathing maneuvers, and while continuing to breathe in this style, take your pulse and/or blood pressure again. With practice, you can become highly skilled at lowering both your heart rate and your blood pressure with only a couple of Deep Sigh Breaths. In time you only need one Deep Sigh Breath because you know how to operate your own body!

A more advanced goal is to feel the sinking, slowing down feeling inside you — like you're going towards sleep — as you do the exhale and rest. You cultivate that by letting go more and more. The slowing down feeling is your parasympathetic nervous system, your body's calming mechanism, engaging. You can relax yourself into soothing sleep.

Another even more advanced goal is to feel your heartbeat inside of your body, either directly or with a finger on your pulse. Feel how your heartbeat quickens as you inhale and slows down as you exhale and rest. Finally, feel when your heartbeat begins to increase again while you are resting. This is your body's signal to start inhaling again.

Emotional Calm – Treasure #1

How to operate your Sympathetic Nervous System

Deep "Sigh" Breath

How to Begin

STEP 1: Deep Inhale	Inhale deeply and smoothly through your nose, filling your entire lungs from the lower abdomen through rib cage to shoulders.
STEP 2: Passive Release	Exhale through your nose by letting go, like a sigh, so the air comes out naturally at its own pace – without forcing or controlling.
STEP 3: Rest	After exhaling, rest as long as you comfortably can – not forcing it – until your body feels it's time to breathe in again. Feel inside for your signal.

How to Practice

Do 3 to 6 Deep "Sigh" Breaths and rest after each exhale. Soothing calm sooner is your goal.

17

INNER PEACE

Uplifting Treasure #2

Para-Sympathetic Nervous System

You have — already built into you — a natural calming mechanism.

This is your para-sympathetic nervous system. All you need to do is turn it on to gain its delightful, highly valued treasure mode. With this skill, you can also keep it on all day for maximum health that conserves your energy and helps keep your blood pressure low.

Your autonomic or involuntary nervous system has two main parts. One arouses and the other calms. You can now choose which one you want with these skills. A stressed out sympathetic nervous system arouses the ancient survival reaction of stress called 'fight or flight'. When the SNS is dominant, the calming part is dormant. Establishing emotional calm with the Deep Sigh Breath serves to quiet the SNS. Now your body's calming mechanism can more fully activate.

It's one thing to be able to feel calm. It's another to have calm as your foundation. With your PSNS turned on, your internal organs can enjoy smoother operating, like a finely tuned engine that hums as it runs. You are healing, building energy, rejuvenating and slowing aging. This is why doctors prescribe 'rest'.

Spiritually, turning on your PSNS opens your body to a greater flow of your life energy. This improved energy circulation uplifts your health and your awareness to new levels. When calm, your physical tissues can receive their most health-producing signals far more easily from your energy skin, the coherent field of electromagnetic energy around you.

Quieting the 'noises' of your body with inner peace also deepens the receiving of uplifting awareness in forms like intuition, insight and creativity at the heart of all meditation techniques.

By stabilizing your breathing style into diaphragmatic or stomach breathing, **resting after each exhale**, you keep your autonomic nervous system at its healthiest throughout the day. This literally prevents anxiety and panic attacks — and can relieve high blood pressure by resetting your Autonomic Nervous System to lower arousal — because you're keeping the SNS turned down. You are conserving energy. Many people with hypertension discover that in time their blood pressure lowers naturally.

Diaphragmatic breathing is also the essential foundation for several types of 'longevity breathing' techniques known to wisdom traditions around the world. Properly done, each breath massages many of your internal organs as we're designed to do. Stomach, small intestines, large intestines, bladder, kidneys, pancreas, spleen — all are continuously massaged all day long.

Happy organs!

You can also consciously direct the energy of the air you inhale to specific organs and body parts, including your brain. Missing from Western medicine, there are ancient 'sciences' for the voluntary control of breathing that are designed to achieve specific health benefits.

Inner Peace – Treasure #2

How to operate your body's calming mechanism: ParaSympathetic Nervous System

Small Stomach "Sigh" Breath

How to Begin

STEP 1: Normal Inhale	Inhale smoothly through your nose, keeping your chest "let go" and letting the inhaled air fill your lower abdomen and expand your stomach outward.
STEP 2: Passive Release	Release your breath through your nose – like a "sigh" with the stomach. Let the air come out as its own natural pace.
STEP 3: Rest	After exhaling, rest as long as you comfortably can – not forcing it – until your body tells you it's time to breathe in again. Focus inside to feel your signal.

How to Practice

STEP 1: Do 3 to 6 Deep "Sigh" Breaths and rest after each exhale.
STEP 2: Do 20 plus Small Stomach "Sign" Breaths and rest after each.

- **Challenge yourself** — let go and relax as much as you can within these 26 breaths.
- **Cultivate the "letting go" feeling** — because that is the direct mechanism for activating your parasympathetic nervous system's calming mechanism. This dissolves fight/flight stress reactions.
- **Gain maximum health benefit** — check your breathing all day long. If you're chest breathing or holding your breath, remedy that with a single **Deep "Sigh" Breath** and then a few **Small Stomach "Sigh" Breaths**.
- **Enjoy your health goal** — help your body make this diaphragmatic breathing style become your normal, regular way of breathing all day – because it is most healthy.

18

PHYSICAL RELAXATION

Uplifting Treasure #3

Skeletal Muscle System

Relax.

How many times have we heard that sage advice, but we just didn't know how to?

Your skeletal muscle system gives you strength, mobility, endurance, lymphatic circulation and... tension. From stomach knots, headaches, back/neck/shoulder pains to teeth grinding and restless fidgeting, a stressed out SMS can deliver incredible amounts of discomfort. In addition to pulling blood flow away from your internal organs to fuel intense life-or-death survival reactions, your skeletal muscles can also store past traumas deep within their fibers.

Like a zip file containing the entire painful experience, muscles can 'record' our emotional memories, good and bad. Many people receiving muscle massages can re-experience ancient life events, which can then be released.

Learning how to feel and rapidly release muscle tension is a health treasure that also improves circulation of blood, oxygen and nutrients. The ability to relax muscles is a necessary complement to strengthening them with exercise, weights and stretching. Physical relaxation is one of the most delicious sensations we can enjoy.

Relaxing is also an energy-conserving, focus-improving vehicle that literally removes physical distractions of discomfort from eating up our limited attention capacity.

The best athletes value using their muscles wisely, never wasting precious energy by keeping muscles unnecessarily tensed. Mohammed Ali brilliantly championed the ability to stay relaxed even during the most intense boxing battles. By doing so, he outlasted many opponents while keeping his reactions brilliantly fast. He didn't have to first relax any tensed arm muscles to then throw a punch. By keeping his muscles relaxed until needed, his speed was blinding.

Practice active muscle relaxation first sitting down or lying in bed for fuller relaxation. Your goal for each muscle group is to FEEL your 'levers' for tensing and use those same 'levers' to release more and more fully throughout each 10 second relaxation period after tensing. Once you can feel how you are letting go with each release lever, then you can quickly relax any and all of your skeletal muscles simply by focusing on releasing without having to first tense! That is what you will do in the second exercise of passive relaxation. You simply focus and let go.

Throughout your day, you can check in to see if you're tensing any muscles unnecessarily — especially jaw and shoulders — and then release them. A great way to fall asleep more easily at night is to focus on releasing your face muscles — jaw, cheeks, eyes and forehead.

Keeping your face muscles relaxed is important because our major sense organs are all located on our face. This means the neurological connections are very intimate between our face muscles and our mental activity. Relaxing your face muscles quiets the mind quickly. If you combine this with the Small Stomach Sigh Breathing, resting and letting go more and more with each exhale while staying focused in the present (not thinking), you'll soon bore yourself into a deep, nourishing sleep.

Physical Relaxation – Treasure #3

Skeletal Muscle System

Active Muscle Relaxation

STEP 1: Tense each muscle group for 5 seconds to feel each of them clearly.
STEP 2: Release each muscle group more and more during a full 10 seconds.
Start at the feet and work up the body — first tensing then fully releasing each muscle group.

1. **feet/calves —** bend your ankles to try to touch your toes to your shin.
2. **thighs —** using only your thigh muscles, straighten your legs, keeping feet and calves let go.
3. **buttocks —** squeeze your buttocks together.
4. **stomach —** tighten or brace your stomach as if resisting someone trying to push it in.
5. **arms/hands —** make a fist with your thumbs outside while tensing your entire arm.
6. **shoulders —** push your shoulders straight up to your ears (not forwards or backwards).
7. **neck stretch —** push your shoulders back and push your chin up and out at a 450 angle.
8. **mouth/jaw —** with teeth apart, force a big smile.
9. **eyes/cheeks —** squinch your eyes tightly shut using your cheeks muscles too.
10. **forehead —** push your eyebrows up as high as you can.

Passive Muscle Relaxation

Without moving anything, start at your forehead and go down your body, feeling and releasing each of your muscle groups more fully — just by feeling how to let go even more deeply with each muscle release 'lever'. You gain success by letting go of each muscle group so it is resting only by its own weight. Challenge yourself to let go more thoroughly and quickly.

- Memorize the feeling of how to let go of your muscles.
- Improve your ability to relax by feeling each release lever.
- Enjoy the comfort and health your body brings you by letting go.

1. **forehead** – slightly raise your eyebrows to feel them, and then release to feel their weight.
2. **eyes/cheeks** – find the position of your eyeballs where they are most relaxed and comfortable and let them rest there without movements. (This is wonderful for quieting the mind to fall asleep).
3. **mouth/jaw** – feel the weight of your jaw, release any tension especially from your jaw's back hinge and let your jaw rest comfortably by its own weight.
4. **shoulders** – feel the weight of your shoulders resting comfortably by their own weight, let go.
5. **arms/hands** – let go to feel the weight of your arms and hands on whatever they are resting.
6. **stomach** – relax your stomach by using the Small Stomach Sigh Breaths.
7. **thighs** – let go more to feel the weight of your thighs on whatever they are resting.
8. **calves/feet** – let go more to feel the weight of your feet upon the floor or on whatever they are resting.

How to Practice for Nourishing Relaxation

STEP 1: Do 6 Deep 'Sigh' Breaths, resting after each exhale.
STEP 2: Do Active Muscle Relaxation up your body.
STEP 3: Do Passive Muscle Relaxation down your body.
STEP 4: Relax more deeply with 20 Small Stomach 'Sigh' Breaths.
STEP 5: Let all your muscles release more and more with each exhale and rest.

Gain the Healthy Benefits of Relaxed Readiness

- Check your muscles frequently throughout the day. If tensed, release.
- Nourish yourself with soothing, rejuvenating muscle relaxation 1-2 times daily.
- Restore healthy circulation of blood, oxygen and nutrients by relaxing.

19

PRESENCE OF MIND

Uplifting Treasure #4

Central Nervous System

Awareness Quantity

Our human capacity to focus our attention seems to be mechanically limited, quantity-wise, to around seven things at once, give or take a couple.[33] That's likely why phone numbers were limited to their seven main numbers, not including area codes.

A single thought can completely fill our focus, and often does, excluding everything else — especially the capacity to pay attention to our driving while texting. Multi-tasking adds to the number of foci, but subtracts from the thoroughness of our awareness in each.

Awareness Quality

Because of this known restricted quantity, ancient wisdom traditions have developed focusing tools and techniques to grow the QUALITY of our awareness. Awareness quality is cultivated by placing our focus in a certain, very specific location within the time-space continuum. We call this 'the present'. Yet it functions to open a gateway or channel for a most important vital flow.

Of what?

Presence of Mind tunes you to ever-expanding layers of fuller awareness. By 'being' in the present, you connect with reality — within and without. You join Life. Your life.

You become the present tense living 'Being' you are — instead of focusing mentally in the past as a human 'was' or in the future as a human 'wanna be'. Most people are not really in the present throughout their day because their mind is full of past and future type thoughts — hence more stress.

Here's how to access the timing of being alive.

Your central nervous system gives you the key to the kingdom of 'being' — awareness, perception, consciousness, intuition, creativity and far more. It seems like an oasis to even briefly stop the devastation of anxiety, panic, worry, racing thoughts, overwhelm, insomnia from an overactive mind, nervousness, negativity, catastrophic thinking and poor concentration. Those unhealthy mental activities are precisely what keeps triggering your HPA-axis survival reactions, hundreds of times daily, so disease development from stress keeps on keeping on.

Once again, health and joy are our guides, forcibly 'guiding' us as individuals and as a species to gain control over our focusing and put an end to creating our own mental misery.

> **With this skill, you can easily clear your mind in seconds, whenever you want.**

As humans, we have learned how to focus our awareness into our past to remember things, good and bad. We can plan ahead by focusing beyond our present time into a potential future, both horrible and wonderful.

But… the timing of life itself is NOW, in the present.

'Stress' today is caused from focusing our mind outside the present — mainly regretting the past and fearing the future — and doing so enough to trigger our HPA-axis as if those scary thoughts are real. But in the present, there is simply 'what is'. We are free from reactivity as long as we remain in the present — continuously aware of what's going on AS it is happening.

In a real life-or death survival situation, we want our fight/flight reaction on to give us its energy, focus and mobility. That is different from being 'stressed out'.

While clearing the mind of 'thinking' seems to be a nearly unattainable goal for so many people, and can take scores of minutes for even experienced meditators to achieve, this challenge is due to our currently dangerous misalignment with reality itself.

Life is alive. Life is not a mental concept.

Entire spiritual traditions are based on cultivating this single treasure. Why?

Here's the big secret: there is no stress in the present.

The present is the timing key for being alive. Life happens NOW. The present is our existential home base in time. We are safe at home in the present. This is a remarkable recognition, infinitely important and profoundly powerful.

Awareness is an extraordinary phenomenon. When you consider 'what' you are being aware of, 'when' you are being aware, you can experience an immediate shift into your larger 'self'. When you ride this awareness of what you are aware of — like a wave of all the information your ears, eyes and skin are continuously bringing to you — you connect with your surroundings in an interesting way.

Once you can hold that focus so you're tuned into the present time — as it is happening — you can become more and more and more aware.

Native spirituality has beautifully illustrated this with four concentric circles. These reflect the awareness of how we grow our 'being'.

Awareness of Our Being

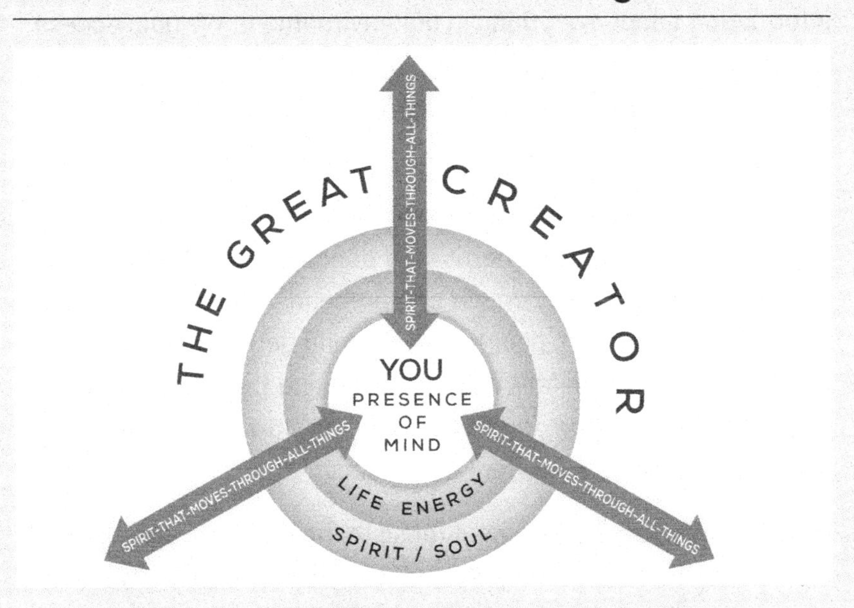

This is an adaptation of a Native American teaching of spiritual reality. With increasing presence of mind, we can expand the awareness of our being beyond the five physical senses into the realms described as Life Energy, Spirit/Soul and more consciously with the Great Creator. All authentic wisdom traditions value awareness in the present as our home base in time, and the foundation for spiritual development. But today most people are 'stressed out' of the present, living with a greatly restricted awareness of fuller being. Fortunately, we can tune into the communications of the Great Creator, which are provided continuously throughout all realms via what is called the 'Spirit-that-moves-through-all-things'. Each of these circles have many levels within them, which means we are able to progress abundantly, for ever and ever. It's a useful map for growing our awareness.

The innermost circle is 'you'. Most people do not even fill that inner circle with their awareness because they are so rarely in the present. When you can accomplish the Presence of Mind skill, you easily fill that circle of awareness. But it is a small circle. The quantity of our focus is limited, like being in a wonderful but tiny bubble.

As we grow our awareness and reclaim emotionally fragmented parts of ourselves, we can expand our awareness of 'being' into the next circle. This is the realm of life energy. It carries enormous information about everything in our environment. We gain access to that information as we develop our focus and reduce the distractions of our body's discomforts.

The next circle is considered the spirit realm. This is where non-physical 'beings' live. While indulging there can be endlessly fascinating, it can also be horrifically dangerous when people try to enter into realms they do not comprehend. Countless cases of mental illness are from people entering and getting stuck in the spirit realm without safety, without protecting themselves and without the knowledge of how to exit cleanly so no spirit level parasites attach to them from that realm.

Wisdom traditions have refined these techniques but teach only those who are capable, humble and who have successfully learned the correct foundational tools. This can take many years and more. Finding teachers who are genuine and willing to train you is another challenge. All wisdom traditions have their methods of qualifying potential students according to their sincerity, capability and worthiness. It's not for everyone.

According to Native spirituality, the final circle is the realm of the Great Creator. Because it is far too powerful and pure for anyone to fully enter that realm while in human form and live, there is what is called: 'the-spirit-that-moves-through-all-things'. This is the flow of the Energy of Life from the Great Creator throughout all the realms. This non-physical stream constantly carries awareness, guidance, intuition, creativity, innovation and solutions to those who can tune themselves into its flow. Doing so is a prized achievement. All cultures have their forms of such 'divination' tools to tune in.

Each of these circles have many levels within them, which means we are able to progress abundantly, for ever and ever. It's a useful map for growing our awareness.

The goal is to tune ourselves in ways that we connect with, receive and accurately interpret the content of the Energy of Life. This is the flow we want more and more of.

The key is to distinguish between focusing internally and focusing externally. 'Thinking' can be described as focusing internally, making pictures in our head, talking to ourself and feeling sensations like emotions inside our body. All these are 'internal' perceptions. 'Thinking' is what causes our stress. We want to be able to instantly stop thinking and start 'perceiving'. These are two different sensory modes.

To clear our mind, we go 'external'. We focus on hearing, seeing and feeling all that is going on around us, but without reacting and judging. We simply observe and notice what is going on AS it is happening. Doing this is quite nourishing because we are 'being' ourself. We are the 'being' who is doing the perceiving. We're alive, tuning in to the vibrant flow of living. Life is a verb. We are living 'beings' alive in the present.

Presence of Mind is the gatekeeper for expanding our awareness.

Presence of Mind – Treasure #4

Central Nervous System

Six Main Sensory Modes

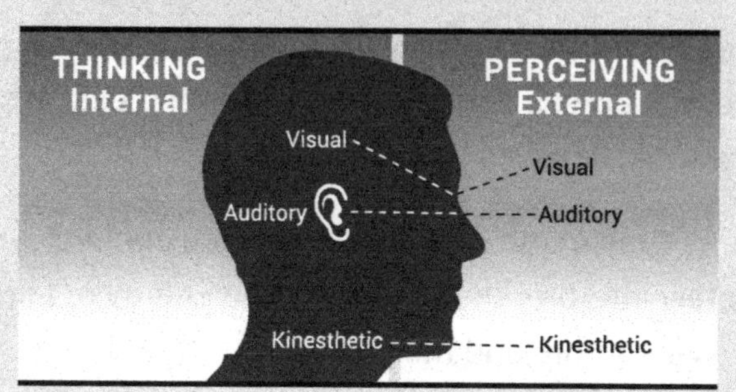

How to Begin

STEP 1: Focus in the auditory external sense	Listen to all the sounds going on around you AS they happen. Ride the sound wave for 30-60 seconds to stabilize your awareness so you are continuously in the present.
STEP 2: Focus in the kinesthetic external sense	Feel with your skin all the sensations touching your skin over your whole body at once, while keeping auditory external focus. Then add feeling the space 3 feet around your body in every (all six) directions.
STEP 3: Focus in the visual external sense	Open your eyes. Notice everything you are seeing – as you are seeing – while also hearing and feeling.
STEP 4: Focus in all three external senses at once	Nourish yourself with greater aliveness by joining the living world around you.

How to Practice

- **Quickly activate** all three external senses at the same time.
- **Enjoy being** in this state for the next 2 to 3 minutes.
- **Play with keeping** your focus external, especially your awareness of sounds around you, while walking and in your routine activities.
- **Check your focus** often all day. Come into the present more and more.
- **To quickly fall asleep:** Utilize the external auditory focus while you let go with your muscles and sink into the bed more and more with each exhale and rest from a few **Deep "Sigh" Breaths** and then **Small Stomach "Sigh" Breaths**. Enjoy letting go into sleep.

20

DYNAMIC CALM

The Uplifting Treasure Mode

Life has sped up. We no longer have the luxury of taking 45 minutes or more to quiet our mind just to then begin an actual meditation. We can do this within six seconds.

Quieting our mind is only the beginning goal of meditation, not the end goal. The more ambitious but authentic goal is to open the flow of the Energy of Life and gain access to its grander awareness.

You can now put the four health treasure skills together to give you the healthy state of calm in seconds. And you can do so while walking, working, driving and computing. This is called Dynamic Calm. You make it yours by practicing this skill until you can apply it easily whenever you want.

You stop living in constant fear and anxiety by establishing your HPA-axis health.

Dynamic Calm is THE #1 health skill for the 21st century.

With this skill you eliminate stress damage before it can develop and you can enter the zone of greater awareness in the present. By aligning all four major body systems into their uplifting 'treasure mode' together, your body naturally enters — in seconds — the ancient prized body/mind state called meditation. This valued state results in your being more alive and better receiving the guidance which the Energy of Life delivers. At the same time, this inner alignment IS the healing state of 'rest', which doctors prescribe to help accelerate the recovery and recuperation from nearly all illness issues.

Your body will love you.

Yet this 'treasure mode' state achieves even more amazing benefits. It establishes something quite desirable and extremely uplifting at the energy level — a very special wave.

Dynamic Calm – The Six Second Skill

How to Combine All the Skills Into a Single Deep "Sigh" Breath

How to Begin	
STEP 1: Deep "Sigh" Breath Inhale	While deeply inhaling through your nose, set your intention to feel calm and focus in the kinesthetic external sense to feel what is touching your skin all over your body all at once.
STEP 2: Passive Release	Combine the momentum of the exhale with the muscle release levers to create a wave of muscle relaxation from forehead to feet in one breath.
STEP 3: Rest and Listen with Presence of Mind	Keep your muscles in the "let-go" position and focus in the auditory external sense as well as the kinesthetic and visual external senses. By resting after the exhale while listening to external sounds and feeling the space three feet around your body in every direction, you immediately increase your awareness and enhance your healthy contact with reality.

How to Practice

As soon as you sense your opportunity awareness signal (formerly know as 'stress'), you can perform the six second Dynamic Calm skill to restore health to your HPA-axis and prevent any potential stress damage. By quickly coming into the present with calm, you can become more aware of the message and the opportunity that your awareness signals communicate to you.

Instead of being 'stressed out', you become a detective in a health-enhancing adventure. You can ride bigger, better energy waves!

Our Two Primary Modes of Purposeful Neurological Organization

The ability to quickly flip our four major body systems into Dynamic Calm in seconds may be today's most important health skill to generate the essential physiological foundation for optimal health and stop the dangerous chronic disease development mode we casually call 'stressed out'.

SURVIVING MODE Defense Physiology		**UPLIFTING MODE** Growth Physiology
Stress Symptoms	**Four Main Body Systems**	**Dynamic Calm Treasures**
anxiety – worry overwhelm – panic **+**	CENTRAL NERVOUS SYSTEM	Presence of Mind **+**
fear – anger – diabetes obesity – hypertension **+**	SYMPATHETIC NERVOUS SYSTEM	Emotional Calm **+**
indigestion sexual dysfunction **+**	PARASYMPATHETIC NERVOUS SYSTEM	Inner Peace **+**
tension – headaches reduced blood flow to internal organs	SKELETAL MUSCLE SYSTEM	Physical Relaxation
= **DISEASE DEVELOPMENT**		= **OPTIMAL HEALTH**

21

QUANTUM SEX

The Wave You Seek

Let's talk about waves.

Unbeknownst to all but a very few physicists, there is no tiniest particle.

The 2400 year old concept of a smallest physical thing that is THE building block of all matter was first called an 'atom' by Democritus in ancient Greece, or perhaps by his teacher, Leucippus. Physicists have been trying to find it ever since.

Spending billions of dollars on super-colliders, the best evidence of a tiniest particle is in the quantum realm — where such things as quarks, bosons, and other exotica have never been seen, but are theorized into being — by the tiniest of momentary possibilities of a shadow of their conjectured existence. Not exactly solid.

Einstein did not buy into the existence of a tiniest physical whatever. Why? Because he knew that the most important challenge for physics to explain is how energy and information are exchanged. A solid physical object, no matter how minuscule and nanoscopic, does not exchange energy.

It turns out that neither Newtonian physics nor quantum physics can explain how energy and information are exchanged.

Fortunately, quantum biology can — simply by understanding one thing:

The tiniest particle of matter is not a particle. It's a wave.

It's waves — all the way down — and all the way up. According to quantum biology, the tiniest aspect of physical reality is a wave structure that has three parts: an in-wave, a spin and an out-wave. Done! This most basic phenomenon is everywhere, at all levels of reality.

The Wave Structure of Matter

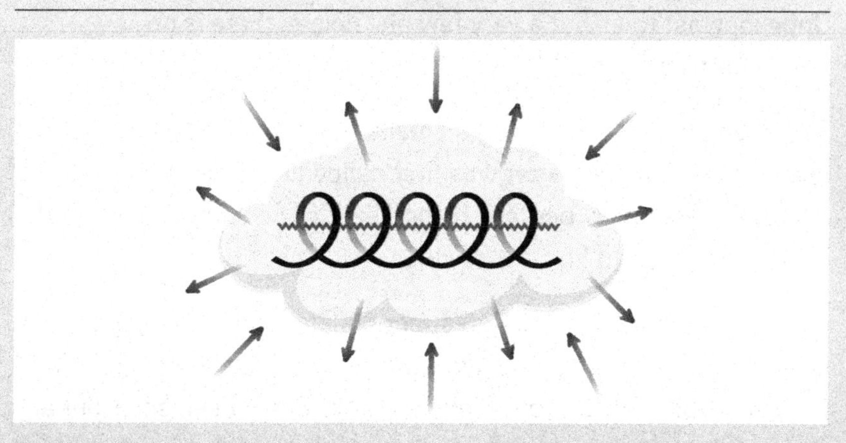

Physicist Milo Wolf, PhD, in his book: *Schrodinger's Universe – Einstein, Waves & the Origin of the Natural Laws*, describes with wonderful elegance the wave structure of an electron, which is a tiny cloud of energy that nobody has seen. This tiniest aspect of physical reality has three parts: an in-wave, a spin and an out-wave. Spherical waves in quantum space converge and diverge from a wave center, where the inward waves change direction and rotate to become the outward waves. This rotation produces the mysterious 'quantum spin', which is how energy and information are exchanged. This most basic phenomenon is everywhere, at all levels of reality.

What does that mean for stress, illness and health? It's all about signals. Health signals carry and deliver their information for health with waves — of energy — which we can greatly expedite once we understand how they work.

What do all forms of meditation, relaxation, healing and rest have in common?

They all remove distractions and 'noise' from both our mind and our body. Why?

Their shared goal is to increase the quality of our focusing — its depth and breadth — so that we can tune our awareness to connect with what is considered a 'higher' form of perception — an elevated consciousness.

How does this work?

Our 'thinking' slows and stops altogether so our mind becomes and remains clear in the present. Our muscles release tension and relax. Our blood pressure lowers and our heart rate slows. The activity level of most of our internal organs slows, quiets and harmonizes. Inner noise quiets. It's as if we expand our 'inner space'.

What does this expansion of inner space accomplish?

It creates the 'space' for something valuable to enter. It invites 'in-waves'. Not just any in-wave, but those of elevated awareness.

It's like your mind is traveling inside a walled garden, through layers and layers of barriers to get to the beautiful opening at the garden's center. Each layer has its challenges to overcome, and that's how each layer provides you with the gifts to see more, hear more and feel more. When you arrive at the center, YOU are more.

Given that healthy signaling IS the core of health, we want to really boost our ability to receive and accurately interpret the health signals that our cells, tissues, glands and organs need.

What improves signaling?

While the foundations of a healthy lifestyle — exercise, nutrition, sleep, calm, joy, love, fun — all improve and uplift signaling, we have yet to activate the energy level nutrients that further enhance and optimize signaling. This is quite important because the actual information being delivered for optimal health is encoded within — and delivered by — energy waves.

For example, good cellphone reception allows the digitally encoded text, email, video and phone call content to be clear and accurate. Poor reception — deteriorated by distance, interference, signal quality or inability to interpret well — can cause serious problems.

There is a fascinating zone where new information carried by signals is taken in — like an approaching ocean wave — that washes over and mixes interactively with whatever is already in that central space. That mixing is the 'spin'. Then the new mix becomes an out-wave that splashes out, carrying its newly combined information to other cells, tissues and organs.

Merging the new with what is already there describes learning at many levels. This is what the 'spin' part of energy waves accomplishes. What optimizes this learning?

A beautiful and ancient way exists at the energy level to improve healthy signaling and do so at all levels of your body. All you have to do is to create in your body a special kind of energy wave.

Bio-physics, also called quantum biology, can describe inner calm as a 'Minimal Amplitude Wave' or MAW.[34, 35] The MAW is the energy activity of the 'spin' that optimizes information uptake and energy exchange. Understanding this process may well change science, technology and healthcare for the better.

You can do now this, because Dynamic Calm establishes your body's dominant energy wave to be this prize. By design, effective meditation also functions to accomplish this.

Each organ, each body system and each cell has its own equivalent mode for a Minimal Amplitude Wave. Just like getting vitamins into your blood uplifts your health, getting the flow of energy with its nutritious information and purposeful guidance uplifts your body systems by keeping them in communication with their greater whole.

One way to understand spontaneous energy healings by people who are considered 'healers', is that the best of them can make the energy field of another person coherent — smooth and calm — so that energetic signals can deliver their operating instructions for continuous optimal health. Dramatic healing can result just by restoring signal reception.

The healer can use energy to create a MAW in the electromagnetic field of the person, or in a specific part of the person's body that is the troubled area. Some healers can also first remove and dissolve the energy level blockages that prevent receiving health signals. In a way, psychotherapy can be thought of as resolving and dissolving the blockages of emotional traumas, false and non-useful beliefs. Then more up-to-date, useful and uplifting beliefs can enter that are reality-based.

A second step for healing is to then be able to direct the Energy of Life into that person — once their field is receptive and can hold the healthier energy. That energy, if pure, delivers the healthiest instructions to all the body's cells, glands, tissues and organs.

When you can do this to yourself, you can stay healthy longer and feel better whenever you want. This is 'Energy Health'. It refreshes at entirely new and important levels.

The future of healthcare will utilize energy devices that accomplish these two conditions and more. First we want to identify the larger coherent energy waves that promote healthy signaling. Once we can establish Minimum Amplitude Waves with our body/mind, we can successfully tune our HPA-axis to better receive. We become open to receiving new, higher level information from bigger and better in-waves.

Next we want to further tune ourselves to invite the best in-waves that uplift.

Remembering that our focus directs energy, we now want to fine tune our focus to direct uplifting energy into us. One super special way of focusing operates as both a receiver and broadcaster of uplifting.

What is this?

22

GENIUS FOCUS

Uplifting Your Mind

While a compass has 360 degrees, and we can walk in any direction, we humans have only two directions of motivation. So far, we've only utilized the second best one.

Historically, the all-pervasive motivation for humanity has been that of survival. Our behaviors seek to get away from, reduce, prevent and eliminate our near constant focus on dangers, worries, problems or worst case scenarios — all the stuff of survival that we do not want.

Motivationally, this is the 'Law of Repulsion'.

But... energetically, because our focus directs energy and our energy broadcasts its content, this actually operates as the 'Law of Attraction'.

> **What we focus on always communicates what we want to our Earth Mother, the living energy matrix of our biosphere that co-creates our physical reality.**

Quite parallel is how our unconscious mind works, again demonstrating the wisdom tool: *as above, so below; as within, so without*.

It's hugely helpful to realize that we cannot process 'words of negation' with our unconscious mind. This means words such as 'no', 'none', 'not', 'less' and 'never' have no real meaning. For example, if you are commanded: "Do NOT picture a green giraffe standing on a blue box with a red ribbon around its neck". What happens?

At some level, you see that picture because you cannot 'not'. However, you can refocus after seeing it. The same thing happens when somebody tells you "do not worry". The word 'not' has no meaning to the unconscious mind, so your focus goes directly to 'worry'. Then your conscious mind quickly fills in the details of all the things you can worry about.

> **Our maturing as a species requires accepting the responsibility for what we are communicating with our focus to the living energy matrix of our biosphere.**

We want to be very clear about what we genuinely want.

Going through life on Earth by avoiding the potholes is mere survival. It doesn't uplift. In fact, focusing in the motivational direction of survival weakens our immune system.[36] At the cerebral cortex level of surviving, nearly all of today's stress damage, especially keeping our HPA-axis activated with fight/flight throughout the day, comes from focusing in one way.

What is this?

You can trigger, and you are re-triggering, your HPA-axis stress reactions — including the survival physiology of fight/flight, the upsetting emotions of anger and fear, plus anxiety — just by focusing on anything you don't want, on anything you WANT LESS OF.

This includes the details of your fears, worries, anxieties, frustrations, problems and difficulties, which are the content of your stress.

Most people are doing this hundreds if not thousands of times daily. The health problem is that it keeps the HPA-axis 'ON' all day in the disease development mode because it doesn't have a chance to recover and restore balance before the next thought of a worrisome problem triggers it again. Being in stress mode also keeps our focus there.

While we get fully engaged in the details of whatever issue we're focusing on, the trick is to be aware at this higher level of our neurological organization, the cerebral cortex, so we know which direction of motivation we are focusing within.

Why? Because we want to steer our focus out of the LESS OF survival focus and into uplifting asap. Awareness — having presence of mind — gives us advantage.

But our awareness of this necessity is now endangered.

Living in a 'stressed out' manner that repeatedly triggers our HPA-axis has become normal and acceptable because everybody is doing it. But... it's neither normal, acceptable, healthy, intelligent nor necessary.

We have a better way of focusing that benefits our HPA-axis health.

Remarkably, our second motivation is all about uplifting. It is the Genius Focus.

When we focus our mind in this direction, we naturally move toward what we are focused on: our goals, desires, joys, interests and values. We feel better.

Motivationally AND energetically, this utilizes the 'Law of Attraction' positively.

This uplifting direction of motivation also boosts our immune strength according to the science of psychoneuroimmunology.[37] Thinking in this way produces healthy neuropeptides and neurotransmitters in our brain that help nerve impulses leap across synapses, the gaps between neurons. And these same neuropeptides and neurotransmitters are instantly found throughout our immune system.[38]

Why would we have a specific way to focus our attention that boosts our immune health?

AND delivers creativity, innovation and humor. AND welcomes solutions into our awareness. AND ultimately generates wisdom.

Are we perhaps supposed to actually utilize it?

A clue to its value is that many of the most successful people throughout human history — those who have made fantastic breakthrough solutions, inventions, discoveries and artistic masterpieces as well as those people with contagious exuberance and vibrant joy of being alive — all somehow figured out how to move their mind into this way of focusing AND keep it there.

The Genius Focus provides a new realm of sustainability for humanity — sustaining our focus into uplifting life — to continually nourish the living energy matrix of our biosphere.

Your ability to uplift is made infinitely easier by first stopping the disease development cycle of being 'stressed out'. Dynamic Calm gives you the solid tools to do so within six seconds by flipping your four major body systems into their health treasure modes. Without such a skill set, it's extremely challenging to think happy thoughts while your physiology is in the life-or-death, fight/flight mode of survival, with your mental activity engaged in problems and when your emotions are dominated by anger and fear.

You naturally want LESS OF that entire ordeal.

That package deal of survival is debilitating, degenerating and destructive of life — your life. This has increasingly gruesome consequences because our Earth Mother grows thoughts into things.

Our species overuse of the LESS OF focus has created an energetic autoimmune disease at the quantum field level.

The more we learn about energy and the nature of reality, the more we recognize that healthy focusing is also our responsibility as individuals and as a species.

Our evolution as a species requires we grow the thoughts into things that nourish our Earth Mother. Learning to steer our focus into uplifting and out of surviving is now essential.

WHEN do you shift your focus into uplifting? Whenever your 'opportunity awareness signal' — formerly known as 'stress' — provides you with its notification to uplift.

Our Two Directions of Motivation

Why the Genius Focus is Our Mind's Steering Wheel to Health

SURVIVING MODE	BRAIN AREAS	**UPLIFTING MODE**
WANT LESS OF	Cerebral Cortex (motivation focus)	**WANT MORE OF**
Analyzing/Dissecting Problems	Cerebellum (mental activity)	Creating / Connecting Solutions
Anger / Fear	Limbic System (emotions)	Desire / Love Joy
Fight / Flight	Brain Stem (physiology)	Feed / Breed

The chart above shows our two dominant motivations and how they operate in the four main areas of our brain. These parts of our brain likely evolved over time from the brain stem upwards to the cerebral cortex.

Neurologically, it is likely that these two modes of motivation, both hardwired into us, are mutually exclusive to each other. The left side is the package of stress and its damaging disease development mode. So we need practical, precise skills to enter into the health-generating uplift mode on the right.

> **Our goal is to know how to quickly and easily flip the entire body/emotion/mind/focus/energy of surviving into the motivational direction of uplifting.**

With the Dynamic Calm skills, you have several 'levers' to move into uplifting. Any of the four body systems which are not moved into uplifting have the capability of derailing your uplift back into the disease development mode of 'stressed out'. Being fully and comprehensively into the body/mind state of Dynamic Calm provides you with a solid state foundation from which to launch into uplift.

There are two additional skills or levers to enter uplifting and stop being stuck in survival.

The highest level of your brain's neurological organization is your cerebral cortex. Like a skin surrounding your brain, this part of our human brain structure was the most recent to develop. It affects and can control all the downline systems in your brain. This means your cerebral cortex directs your cerebellum's mental activity, your limbic system's emotions and your brain stem's physiology. We can make good use of this.

What you focus on at the cerebral cortex level directs all your downline brain systems. AND you can control your cerebral cortex with your focus.

> **The good news is that you now have a wonderful, powerful mind-steering wheel!**

Your ability to focus at the cerebral cortex level is your mind-steering wheel. We are designed to have the option to stay stuck in survival or choose to uplift. We can flip our focus into uplifting from that of surviving with... The Big Lever!

> **We steer our focus onto what we WANT MORE OF from focusing on what we WANT LESS OF. This is 'The Big Lever' of our mind.**

Doing so switches us into our Genius Focus. This positively affects all downline systems in our brain.

This simple move is deeply profound. As we cultivate the Genius Focus, we are increasingly and continuously developing new neurological pathways for uplifting. We strengthen our immune system. We repeatedly experience the growth of joy by applying the Genius Focus into every area of our lives, increasingly and continuously.

What is this actually doing?

The Genius Focus opens and grows a most uplifting relationship — between your personality that you consider your 'self' and something much more essential. This is what wisdom traditions call your 'True Self'.

> **You directly communicate — increasingly — with the source of your self-esteem, your self-confidence, your self-respect and your self-love.**

With the Genius Focus, these qualities of a healthy personality can finally take on practical meaning. Let's re-define a few key concepts in psychology based on uplifting instead of survival.

What is 'self-confidence'?

Genuine self-confidence is knowing you have a "Self" that is the source of your guidance, intuition, inspiration and creativity. This aspect has been called many names, like 'higher self', 'soul', 'essential self', 'super ego', your 'center' and more. The names matter less than the knowledge that 'it' has its own reality not limited by any name. But names can be useful as a focusing aid.

The fact that 'it' is there inside you — as the real you — and you can increasingly access its greater awareness for your benefit, is certainly enough to inspire your efforts to connect. Why would you not want to gain access to a wiser part of you that can guide you to best achieve all your goals, desires and joys? The extent you do is related to your self-esteem.

'Self-esteem' is the act of choosing to steer your focus to connect with this source and then valuing the guidance you receive from it — by acting on it. 'Self-love' is simply the act of focusing to connect with this, your essence. You are honoring and loving you.

How?

> **You activate your Genius Focus simply by asking yourself: "What do I want MORE OF?"**

When you begin doing this in every situation, in every relationship, in every moment, you more fully open the communication with the mysterious source that is a top goal of all true wisdom traditions, spiritual paths and effective religions.

An example of its game-changing power is applying the Genius Focus to healthcare. The entire medical system is limited to the LESS OF focus of survival, because it only seeks to reduce or manage illness conditions. Even when successful, it doesn't produce health.

> **Medical students learn about pathology — symptoms, illness and disease — not about growing health.**

What's clearly missing is the entire upper, better half: optimal health. Our healthcare system does not produce optimal health because it doesn't know how. Even illness prevention is similarly limited as a survival-based motivation we want LESS OF — illness.

Focusing on and producing optimal health will easily reduce the vast majority of medical costs because people will be very healthy. We need a parallel to the current disease model, a new one that researches how healthy humans can become and what knowledge, tools and resources literally produce health. From that emerges the means to the goal of an optimally healthy population — nationally and globally.

Applying the Genius Focus to climate concerns is equally disruptive to the status quo mentality. Instead of merely trying to achieve LESS OF pollution or lower carbon emissions, we can focus on what positively nourishes the environment and makes the biosphere optimally healthy. Many areas of life are ripe for uplifting in these ways.

What does our Earth Mother want MORE OF?

Asking is the beginning of wisdom. Receiving delivers the goods.

It's beneficial to ask yourself at any moment which direction are you tuning into. With your Presence of Mind skill, you can be more aware of your direction and increasingly uplift. Here is an exercise to begin applying your Genius Focus into your daily life

The GENIUS Focus

For Uplifting Solutions & Optimal Mind Health

Identify specific things you want **LESS OF** in these life areas and transform each into what you want **MORE OF**.

LESS OF > > > INTO > > > MORE OF

Feelings or Emotions (LESS OF)

1. ______________________________
2. ______________________________
3. ______________________________

Feelings or Emotions (MORE Of)

1. ______________________________
2. ______________________________
3. ______________________________

Values and Experiences (LESS OF)

1. ______________________________
2. ______________________________
3. ______________________________

Values and Experiences (MORE Of)

1. ______________________________
2. ______________________________
3. ______________________________

Thoughts (LESS OF)

1. ______________________________
2. ______________________________
3. ______________________________

Thoughts (MORE Of)

1. ______________________________
2. ______________________________
3. ______________________________

How to Practice and Benefit:

1. **Apply the Genius Focus** to all areas to continually discover how to uplift and improve your life! • thoughts • understandings • feelings • emotions • goals • outcomes • experiences
2. **Identify what qualities you want MORE OF in your:** • job • activities • relationships • communications • behaviors • intentions • life

Producing Optimal Health

A New Direction

Knowledge has advanced beyond the business of healthcare, beyond illness reduction, beyond illness prevention and even beyond wellness. We can now produce optimal health.

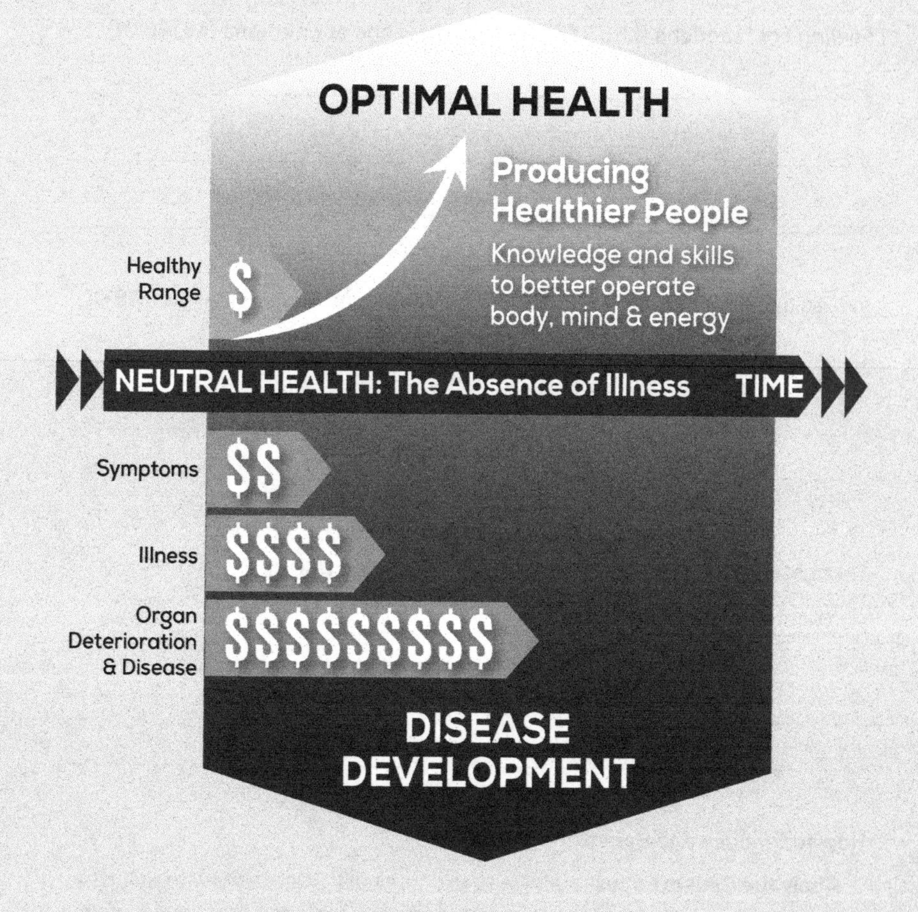

23

YOUR BIG MIND

Why would you want to steer your focus?

If you suspect your life and life on Earth can be better — and you are up for a grander adventure — stay tuned. With the Genius Focus, you can now steer your focus into uplifting. And you can do so increasingly to uplift every area of your life as you continue to discover what you really want more of.

At the body/mind level of health, including your immune system, The Big Lever is massively practical. You can feel the immediate consequences of your focus by simply tuning into your body when stating something from the Surviving Focus and then restating it after using The Big Lever to transform it into the Uplifting Focus.

For example, while feeling inside your body, try saying to yourself: "I want less stress, less anxiety, less depression, less worry, less fatigue and less difficulties." Repeat this a few times until you feel how your body, mood and energy levels are all affected.

Then apply The Big Lever to make that uplifting. While feeling inside your body, say to yourself: "I want more calm, more peace, more joy, more confidence, more energy and more success." Repeat this also a few times until you can feel how your body, mood and energy levels are all affected.

Can you feel the differences? This is how your focus is always affecting you at physical, mental, emotional and immune strength levels. This is how it communicates to the living energy matrix of our Earth Mother.

You can also use the Genius Focus to help others uplift their focus out of a survival mentality. Most arguments, blaming and other forms of negativity and conflict are in the LESS OF focus. Instead of arguing, you can just ask the other person what they want MORE OF, and that you'll help them get that. While this is a simple question, most people will still answer with what they don't want, what they want LESS OF. So it might require asking again, and even describing the difference to people. You're actually doing them a great favor, like teaching a person how to fish.

However, what you are really doing, whether for yourself or others, is at the energy level. Your focus directs energy. Energy delivers content.

To whom or what? What are you aiming your focus to connect with?

When you ask yourself, in YOUR head and in YOUR heart, what YOU want MORE OF, to whom are you talking?

Who is listening? Who knows?

Answering the question of "who knows" is exceedingly uplifting — a continuous pathway for awakening. Is there some storehouse of all your wants? Or is there a core part of you that knows your real wants and might share them with you if you ask respectfully?

Indeed there is.

By combining the Genius Focus with Dynamic Calm — turning on your health treasures of Presence of Mind, Emotional Calm, Inner Peace and Physical Relaxation — you powerfully establish a fascinating body/mind 'state' that uplifts you.

Dynamic Calm **opens gateways** for uplifting in-waves to enter your awareness. Genius Focus **attracts the flow** of these in-waves into you through this gateway of what's continuously 'better'.

This combo widens the flow of energy that delivers communication from the source of your intuition, creativity and guidance. You are inviting a specific in-wave into your awareness from something more aware than you are consciously.

What is this mysterious, extraordinary, phenomenal, uplifting source that is valued throughout the ages by all cultures? In wisdom traditions, spiritual paths and religions, it has many names.

You are tuning IN to your 'Big Mind'.

As the source of your intuition, creativity, guidance and solutions, imagine how vastly more aware your Big Mind must be to provide your conscious mind, your 'little mind', with such valuable communications. What more expansive realms of being can your Big Mind be living in?

Connecting directly with your Big Mind is a prize that all spiritual paths, religions and wisdom traditions originally taught. Doing so has a few initial requirements.

1. You have to know how to quiet your mind.
2. You have to know how to calm your body.
3. You have to know where to place your focus in time.
4. You have to know how to focus inside you.

5. You have to know where to focus inside you to directly connect with your Big Mind.
6. You have to know what to do with your focus inside you to connect with your Big Mind.
7. You have to do it.
8. You have to practice because that's how you gain the experience, skills and awareness your Big Mind gives you to increasingly tune in.

So far you have learned how to do the first four steps in this book. More are coming!

Your Big Mind is home to your uplifting awareness. It is 'awareness central'.

You can use your focus to direct energy — lots of energy — to do many incredible things once you discover for yourself the better uses of your focus and learn its fuller potential.

Using your focus to uplift is by far a great use of your energy, time, efforts and life. Why would you not? Uplifting gives you more of what you really want in many vital areas.

With an energy understanding, you can operate your HPA-axis properly to literally create a better life and a more healthy reality. How?

PART IV:

REALITY – THE GAME WE ARE IN

The interactive quality of life on Earth
exists to teach us humans to grow up
and realize that the content of our focus
attracts its manifestation into physical reality.
As a species, we now can embrace
the amazing possibilities
of focusing together to co-create
our best reality imaginable.

24

THE PURPOSE OF THE LAW OF ATTRACTION

Understanding the nature of reality can amaze and delight!

Your HPA-axis operates as a tuner that both receives and broadcasts.

With Dynamic Calm you are energetically creating a 'Minimum Amplitude Wave', something recent bio-physics has discovered to be the prime condition for transferring both energy and information. This achieves a core purpose of meditation: to receive an in-wave of uplifting guidance, intuition, creativity and solutions from your Big Mind.

Then Minimum Amplitude Waves, after mixing new energy and information, become out-waves. THIS is our impact on the world. It is our communication.

> **As energy broadcasters, we are calling out to the fabric of reality. It responds.**

It is similar to the 'call and response' in African music, singing, dancing and drumming.

But... what is your out-wave? Is it healthful or harmful?

As our human species matures, we must recognize the reality of how important it is to take responsibility for our out-waves. Why? Because we are doing something quite potent that we have yet to even become aware of, much less put to good use.

Simply seeing the state of our world tells us what our species' out-waves are. We have disease, corruption, pollution, contamination, hatred, greed, bigotry, racism, genocides, slavery, wars, extreme climate events, environmental destruction and other survival-era creations like governments constantly funding the development of biological and other new weapons. For what? None of these are needed. None of these nourish life.

You might not see these events as resulting from human out-waves that deliver disgusting content to the fabric of reality. But... they are indeed. This back-and-forth is a key quality of our biosphere reality. It is interactive. A popular name for this is 'karma'.

This is precisely why our species must uplift and evolve into contributing value. We have become powerful focusing beings without a steering wheel and clueless of our destination.

> **The interactive quality of life on Earth exists to teach us humans to grow up and realize that the content of our focus attracts its manifestation into physical reality. We are growing — into being — whatever we are focusing upon whether good or bad, right or wrong, true or false.**

It's that simple.

This awareness is taught in all cultures in forms like: 'you reap what you sow', 'what goes around comes around', The Golden Rule, 'love your neighbor as yourself' and more. But we haven't applied it to our relationship with the environment or to greater wholes.

Taking this responsibility for our out-waves is our next evolutionary marker of our species' maturity. It's like waking up to how the quality of food you put into your mouth either makes you healthy or diseased. Either the food nourishes you with vitamins, minerals, enzymes and physical forms of sunlight; or it contaminates, pollutes, upsets and poisons your body in ways that trigger illness, inflammation, fatigue and dementia.

Additionally, the choices of our food dictate the agricultural methods used to grow them — either nourishing and regenerating the soil — or killing soil's essential living microbes, depleting minerals and destroying nutrients with unhealthy farming methods — which spread further contamination from harmful, cancer-causing chemical pesticides and fertilizers.

The reality of out-waves explains why many pharmaceuticals, if not nearly all of them, cause such damaging side effects. Their focus is on aiming a chemical in-wave into a very specific target at the chemical/molecular level. They are irresponsible for the out-waves that their in-wave creates.

Their out-waves are usually incompatible with the health of surrounding tissues. Wherever their out-waves reach, they likely interfere with healthy signaling. Pharmaceutical companies need to be responsible for their out-waves. Their out-waves must also create health. Out-wave responsibility applies to the entire petrochemical, fossil fuels, plastics and cellphone/microwave industries — all of whom are polluting intensely.

The same is true for our personal out-waves — how the content of the energy directed by our focus affects the fabric of reality. The fabric of reality, Earth's energy 'soil', somehow takes in your energy and its content. It then responds in some way to you personally, feeding back into your reality what you are broadcasting, while also storing in some way the frequencies you have output.

Those frequencies evidently accumulate in ways we don't yet comprehend. We're either tossing garbage into a pile to create a trash dump — into the very fabric of reality on Earth — or we're nourishing the energy garden with life-enhancing nutrients of uplifting thoughts, desires, dreams and feelings that grow life. Either way, these frequencies are associated with us. They become our personal identity, our frequency signature which keeps us aligned with — or stuck with — attracting people, creating experiences and having perceptions of a similar frequency.

To uplift, we can change our frequency 'clothing'.

We are doing this type of reality-creation constantly, albeit mostly unaware of the larger ecosystem we're engaged with. That fuller ecosystem includes the living energy matrix of our Earth Mother.

What is this really?

We are attention-focusing creatures, hybrids with a physical biological body and a non-physical energy 'soul' or spirit. And we are powerful.

As we apply the wisdom tool — *as above, so below; as within, so without* — we can usefully think of ourselves as super exotic plants. We grow flowers, fruits and blossoms into the biosphere of our Earth Mother with our focus and our actions.

When we apply this as a species with benevolent purpose, all life on Earth rejoices.

What fruit should we be growing? What fruit is absolutely best for life on Earth?

For that answer, we have to ask our Earth Mother herself. She knows. Let's ask her.

25

THE LIVING MATRIX

Our Earth Mother's Soul

We generally accept the concept that we have a 'soul' — a longer lasting, grander, non-physical larger being — that is actually the real 'us'. Certainly, every culture, every religion and every spiritual tradition acknowledge this with a variety of names and descriptions.

At the energy level, it can be imagined as an organizing pattern, like a value, but far more powerful. Except, unlike the values we create, it is the actual living, aware director of our entire life. It directs us to achieve its designated purposes. It manifested itself as 'us' into a physical body, but as a smaller, less aware part of itself. As magnificent as we are, compared to our 'soul', our entire body is akin to a single leaf on its large tree.

A traditional wisdom metaphor is that each of our various lifetimes in all our existences is like one leaf among many leaves on a tree. The leaves are always receiving nutrients for life from the center of the tree trunk, which can be considered the 'soul'. The entire tree with all its leaves, branches and limbs is considered our total 'entity'. Not limited by linear thinking, our soul can create more than a single leaf to be living at the same time. Meeting another person who is a leaf from your same soul tree could be interesting.

Your tree might also be next to many other trees, whose branches overlap and touch. These are people in your soul 'family' who seem to re-appear in many of your lifetimes.

We can say that this soul level of our being is the Big Mind source of our intuition, creativity, inner guidance and more. Compared to us, our soul level of being is super alive. Constantly guiding us throughout our lives, we are rather like its puppets on a leash that gives us some free will. Our soul has purpose for creating and guiding us, often referred to as our 'life mission'.

Having a higher purpose is another source of joy. Knowing this purpose and living it brings even richer meaning to our lives.

But whether we listen and learn to tune in to its guidance is another issue. We can wander off track, but eventually the consequences will wake us up, like a midlife 'crisis'.

Or stress.

While we generally accept this arrangement as true for humans, it seems unnecessarily challenging to comprehend that this planet, our Earth Mother, is also a living being AND she has the equivalent of a 'soul'. Her soul is the actual matrix, the living energy level of 'being' that forms and sustains her physicality.

Scientists might think of this as the quantum field of earth, as its organizing blueprint, but without yet recognizing its aliveness and consciousness as a being.

> **Any human who cannot see our Earth Mother as a living being either has a very small mind, or has not wondered.**

Choosing to believe otherwise is typically justified in order to pillage her or to make money — carelessly ignoring the damage to her body and harm to the health of her being.

While turning on her axis and rotating around the sun, fed energy by continuous solar winds, with molten iron churning in her core, her elements of air, water, soil and fire are circulating constantly. All biological life interacts, transforming into new life forms and new ecosystems that wax and wane non-stop from her elements with elaborate cycles of growth, decay and rejuvenation on her surface.

All these are sure indicators of a living being. Is that too much to grasp?

This greater awareness — that the planet we are living within is a living being — is far more joyous. To experience our Earth Mother as alive is a wondrous thing we humans are uplifting into.

We're not living ON Earth. We're living IN our Earth Mother. The skies are part of her being, as is the molten iron churning in her core.

But... the 'soul' of our Earth Mother is best honored, loved, cherished and communicated with, like talking to a dear friend who gives you all you need to live. Wondrous interactive experiences abound with the right attitudes: gratitude and respect.

For our Earth Mother is far more wise and aware than are we as a mere species upon her surface. She absolutely knows what is good for her and for all the biological life she generously grows. We have only the consciousness of a single individual of a single species. Our Earth Mother has the consciousness of an entire planet and all the species in her.

When we humans learn how to 'listen', an ability indigenous peoples have cultivated over millennia, a most marvelous and delightful new dimension of life blossoms for us.

Nemonte Nenquimo, a Waorani woman, mother and leader of her people, wrote in her letter (excerpts here) to the presidents of nine Amazonian countries and to other world leaders:

> *"It took us thousands of years to get to know the Amazon rainforest. To understand her ways, her secrets, to learn how to survive and thrive with her. You are not as complex as the rainforest."*

> *"The forest is my teacher. And I have learned enough to know that you have lost your way, and that you are in trouble (though you don't fully understand it yet) and that your trouble is a threat to every form of life on Earth. You forced your civilization upon us and now look where we are: global pandemic, climate crisis, species extinction and, driving it all, widespread spiritual poverty. In all these years of taking, taking, taking from our lands, you have not had the courage, or the curiosity, or the respect to get to know us. To understand how we see, and think, and feel, and what we know about life on this Earth."*

> *"This forest has taught us how to walk lightly and because we have listened, learned and defended her, she has given us everything: water, clean air, nourishment, shelter, medicines, happiness, meaning. And you are taking all this away, not just from us, but from everyone on the planet, and from future generations. And so I say to you: the Earth does not expect you to save her, she expects you to respect her. And we, as Indigenous peoples, expect the same."* [39]

Modern humans are missing the best, most awesome treasures of our biological reality.

Our Earth Mother gives us all the clues we need to thrive and fulfill our species' magnificent contribution to her biosphere and to the community of living beings.

> **As we tune in with Dynamic Calm to establish a Minimum Amplitude Wave so we can best receive her gifts; and we use our Genius Focus to attract her communications in addition to those of our own 'Big Mind', we shall be flooded with amazing, new uplifting energy and astounding new ideas, creations, inventions, discoveries and solutions.**

These will provide the content for a new global economic reward system based on nourishing life on Earth. Those who can tune in will win!

These clues are so elegant and so blatantly obvious, that we have overlooked their power and wisdom. Imprisoned in their survival-based fear that comes with valuing money and power more than life itself, human "Enemies of Life' have stupidly violated the two most important values for successful life on Earth.

As we align with these two beautiful values that nourish life in the very best ways, and we do so continuously, we accomplish the great UPLIFT.

What are these two values?

26

THE VALUES FOR UPLIFTING

What does money value? Anything?

Money is value-free. It has no values. Everybody values money, but money has no values.[40]

That is a major problem, because money is disconnected from biological reality.

To uplift life on Earth, we have to connect it. But to what?

Money and our entire global economic reward system must serve the biological reality of life's Prime Directive – to nourish life. Once we align money with nourishing life, then money will purposefully serve to blossom genuine value into life. People can still make money, but with new rules. Everyone in the business of making money then simultaneously contributes to making life on Earth better. This economic shift establishes a necessary foundational driver for our uplifting.

Two values can direct the entire evolution of our human species to uplift life on Earth. Like our human values, these are energy-transformers — flow ways that distribute and channel the Energy of Life. Like all values, they also grow new beliefs with supporting principles, information, knowledge, motivation, thought and behaviors.

The values which come to us from the Energy of Life are the values that best nourish, direct, inform and grow life. Functionally, this should be obvious. Re-purposing our entire global economic reward system to accomplish these two values is what we now need to do for a most amazing uplift.

The first value is HEALTH.

This is super-functional. It does it all.

With health as our top value, all our beliefs, thoughts, motivations and actions will be energized with the quest for greater health. This value insures survival — for all. It promotes growth of the best kind. It defines the best quality in every realm of biological life on Earth.

This is the top value our species must now agree upon achieving, so we can collaborate and operate our behaviors collectively for good purpose.

When we do, truly genuine and lasting benevolence can grow here on Earth. Imagine all people, all fish, all animals, all plants, all birds, bees and the entire biosphere of our Earth Mother enjoying fantastic health to the max.

That is our mission.

The value of health comes from an even higher source. This source is the living awareness that knows exactly what best grows all life and life on Earth.

When we can tune ourselves to receive that pure awareness of instructions for health, then phenomenal new uplifting discoveries, innovations, inventions and creations will blossom into new products, goods and services that uplift. That is what our economy must now reward.

To tune in better and make sure their actions were benevolent to life on Earth, indigenous peoples of the Americas made decisions based on how seven generations into the future would be affected. Try thinking like this. It is mind-expanding!

The second value is JOY.

We are guided best by what brings us joy and makes us feel good. Obvious, yes?

But why would there be JOY?

In us hybrid beings, part physical and part non-physical, endowed with emotions that fuel our energy, motivations and guidance system, joy feels great! Why? Joy could have been dismal.

If it was dismal, we would be naturally motivated to move away from it, repelled by its disgusting effects on us. Instead we have joy that feels fantastic throughout its entire delicious range of positive emotions from good to wonderful, fantastic to divine.

Joy feels delightful BECAUSE it is what nourishes life!

Like an organic fertilizer, joy grows the flow of the Energy of Life. Health and joy are our species' simple but true paths to uplifting, evolving and advancing us for the best of biological life.

We are being guided by health and joy to uplift us, and by their opposites to redirect us.

We just have to implement them into our civilization, into our institutions, into our relations and into all areas of our human species' activities. These will produce far superior qualities of life than any values now currently dominant.

Of course life has disappointments, challenges, traumas, catastrophes, hardships, dangers, diseases and difficulties. These survival level experiences are part of our evolutionary process for growth. With these we are given motivations to overcome the problems, solve the challenges, heal the illnesses, improve the safety and become smarter about living on Earth.

But these challenges are always journeys to the real goals of health and joy.

Nearly all stress is from not living in alignment with these real values, but trying to 'get by' spending time, effort and energy with lesser values. Sometimes we have to in order to survive, but it is still the integrity gap between what we value and what we are doing that IS the stress. Stress is damaging in order to get our attention, because it is our awareness signal telling us to uplift — to our highest values — while delivering the content to do so.

Any spiritual path, any religion, any wisdom tradition and any government that does not uplift people into greater health and joy is likely out of touch with the Prime Directive of Life. *We the People of the Earth* have responsibility to fix it.

What do HEALTH and JOY achieve at the energy level?

How do they really function?

27

THE ENERGY OF LIFE

We know that 'everything is energy'. And that includes life itself.

What is the 'Energy of Life'?

What does it do? Where does it come from? How can you get more?

No scientist has yet been able to measure or even describe the 'Energy of Life'. Yet, all logic, evidence and experience makes its existence obvious. We see the effects of this fertilizer of life everywhere.

Life is.

Many older cultures and traditions around the world have developed extensive systems and effective techniques to build, grow and circulate in the human body what is called 'life energy'. In virtually every language, there is a word for this 'life energy'. And nearly always, its second definition is the word 'breath'. Inhaling healthy oxygen and exhaling waste products are like a physical realm analogy for us to understand the importance of bringing healthy energy into our being — continuously.

In Chinese, life energy is called 'qi' or 'chi'. In Japanese and Korean, it is 'ki'. India calls it 'prana'. Hawaii calls it 'ha'. The English word 'spirit' — with its derivatives of 'inspiration' and 'respiration' — comes from the Greek 'spiritos', which means to breathe. That Greek word likely comes from the earlier Hebrew 'sefirot', which has enormous depth.

In Hebrew, the Energy of Life is called 'ruach hakodesh', which literally means 'holy breath'. These are the precise Hebrew words used in Genesis of the Torah, the Five Books of Moses, to describe what the Creator blew into the nostrils of the first human to bestow life. On the human energy spectrum is the Hebrew word 'neshama', which means 'soul'. It is related to 'neshema', a Hebrew word for breath that shares the same essential root letters.

While there is at least one word for life energy in these languages, those who are practitioners understand that there are many levels of this energy, both in quantity and quality. Energy is on a spectrum, a continuum, from the subtlety of an electron to the solidness of a rock and to what we can only describe as the highest, most sublimely 'divine'.

In addition to bringing the Energy of Life into us, we can then do things with it. Older traditions of wisdom around the world teach tools to activate what are called 'energy centers'. These are vortices of moving, spinning or circulating energy 'organs'. Our bodies have several of them. Although their locations in the body and their functions vary among these traditions, there are many shared elements. This commonality is interesting in itself because many of these systems were originally developed — and refined — millennia ago in various parts of the world without collaborating communication.

How?

There are people who have the ability to directly perceive these energy centers. Some people can see them while others can sense or feel them. This validates their existence, even without modern scientific measurement capabilities. Until our species' motivations elevate from mere survival into the benevolence of uplifting, it's probably a good thing that science cannot yet identify these types of energy.

Like connecting dots of energy, a goal of each traditional system is to activate all of these life energy centers together to gain the even higher level functionings of their greater whole. When healthy, each energy center operates to improve, strengthen and nourish the functioning of its related physical organs, glands and more.

> **New levels of health, vitality, awareness, joy, peacefulness, consciousness, wisdom and understanding are some of the many valued benefits from this life energy development.**

Yet without ENERGY JOY's uplifting frequency that stabilizes our guidance, people striving for more and more life energy are in danger of merely feeding energy to amplify their unrefined character traits like narcissism, greed and negativity. This is one reason why, before teaching the secrets of life energy development, the true spiritual/religious/wisdom traditions teach qualities we know as morals, ethics, integrity, generosity, compassion and kindness. These qualities have valuable energetic function as well. They keep our electromagnetic energy field clean of energy debris that blocks ENERGY JOY's higher frequencies as well as interfering with our opportunity awareness signals.

Life energy comes in a spectrum just like the known electromagnetic energy spectrum goes by increasingly shorter wavelengths from radio waves to microwaves to infrared to visible to ultraviolet to X-ray to gamma rays. All these vibrations of energy are part of the electromagnetic spectrum that include electrical energy, heat, sound, light, radio waves and radioactive waves.

The energies throughout the spectrum can deliver content.

Waves of light, frequencies of sound, radio waves and microwaves all bring us encoded information that we can translate into stuff that 'makes sense'. Our digital devices all deliver videos, emails, texts and tweets by encoding content into their carrier waves. Unfortunately, these carrier waves are increasingly all microwaves which have become dangerously disruptive of healthy cell signaling — in humans and throughout Nature — all of which depend on healthy signaling for life.[41]

There is no biological intelligence in that. This is an example of the idiocy that happens when money does not serve the Prime Directive of nourishing life. Such is their obsession with the currently valueless symbol we call 'money'[41] that even though they know its dangerous consequences to life, those promoting microwaves as a communication medium continue contaminating the entire biosphere.

They easily qualify as 'Enemies of Life'.

But what happens as we journey up into the higher, more elevated realms of the life energy spectrum?

We know that energy delivers content. What content does this 'Energy of Life' deliver?

To help our understanding move from the physical realm into the energetic realm, we can always invoke the wisdom tool: *as above, so below; as within, so without.*

In our physical world, the sun seems to be the primary source of the energy that sparks life. When we observe the impact of sunlight, the solar energy waves from our local star, we can recognize a life-stimulating effect upon the surface of the Earth. Sunlight makes things on Earth grow, blossom, sprout and more. Sunlight somehow fosters, directs and sustains life on Earth.

How does it do that?

Most people simply see and feel sunlight without thinking further about it. But for sunlight to stimulate biological life and direct its development, it must also be delivering precious content. We can usefully compare this content to the DNA in our cells. But its nature is not physical.

Light delivers it.

Nobel laureate biochemist Albert Szent-Gyorgi described one beautiful effect of sunlight. When a photon of sunlight interacts with a material particle on Earth, it lifts one electron from an electron pair up to a higher level. This 'excited' state is of very short duration, and the electron quickly drops back to its ground state.[42]

What does this achieve?

This raising and lowering gives off excess energy in some form. Life has learned how to 'catch the electron' in its excited state, uncouple it from its partner and utilize its excess energy for life's processes.[43]

In bio-physics terms, sunlight is an energy 'in-wave' that interacts with matter (via the process of establishing a Minimum Amplitude Wave that delivers its content) and creates an 'out-wave' of energy that nourishes life.

How amazing is that?

This is rather exactly like what happens in our mitochondria, the energy production factories in all our cells. A tri-phosphate molecule called ATP releases one of its phosphate groups to become a di-phosphate molecule called ADP. This release produces our biological energy. The more mitochondria we have in our cells, and the more efficiently they do this, the healthier we are, and the greater our prospects for longevity.[44,45,46,47]

As above, so below; as within, so without —
it's all about energy!

In Nature, living systems are designed to eventually age and disintegrate, called 'entropy', which results in death through energy loss. The opposite of aging and deterioration is the energy regenerating process called 'negentropy'.

Is it possible to reverse aging when you are flowing the actual life-giving Energy of Life into you and through you? This energy certainly rejuvenates and at least slows aging — because you're literally energizing.

You are actually refreshing your life energy, your electromagnetic field, your organs, glands and tissues with higher frequencies of health — while you are cleansing and nourishing your magnetic field, the medium of healthy cell signaling. While there are limits, many physicians and scientists say that our body is designed to live 120 years. The Bible describes many people who lived several hundred years.

Perhaps this leads to the famed 'fountain of youth', which might well be a flow of energy, not something physical like a water fountain.

Miraculously, when the male sperm and the female egg mate, a single-celled embryo forms that contains all the necessary ingredients to produce an adult human.

How might that work?

A physician named Robert O. Becker studied how salamanders re-grow severed limbs. He surmised the existence of an energetic 'blueprint' that directs cell and tissue growth throughout life. He thought this blueprint also forms at the moment when the sperm and egg mate.[48, 49]

Considering the sperm as an 'in-wave' mixing its genes with those genes already in the female egg as 'the spin' and the fertilized egg as the expanding 'out-wave', perhaps our most tangible experience — and reward — for a Minimum Amplitude Wave is the orgasm itself!

Actually, there are ancient wisdom traditions, like Tantric Yoga, that cultivate the orgasm as a sacred experience that connects people to the higher 'in-waves' we call 'divine'. Certainly, there's no shortage of people calling out the Creator's name with joy!

In humans, we continuously grow hair, nails, skin, cells and two sets of teeth — but not severed limbs — yet. It's quite possible as we understand the energetic blueprint, we can learn how to selectively stimulate re-growing any organs we choose — like awakening our own stem cells to do their thing — again.

I recall as a youth reading a Superman comic where little Jor-El was a young child on his home planet Krypton, playing in a tree when he fell and broke his arm. His mother put him inside a phone booth type device in their living room, closed the door and hit the 'GO' button. Three minutes later little Jor-El walked out with his arm fully healed.

This is our future.

All these are fascinating effects of life energy. But what is the actual 'Energy of Life', the higher level form of energy that creates, nourishes, directs and sustains life itself?

What does it deliver? This knowledge is the ultimate prize of all spiritual, religious and wisdom traditions.

Whoever tastes, knows.

Ready to taste?

28

THE JOY ENGINE

Your Energy Heart

Before the existence of physics terms and our current scientific understandings, many ancient texts — especially religious, spiritual and writings that are considered sacred — have described energy in a variety of ways.

English translations of the Bible frequently use the word 'countenance' to describe someone's energy field, like: 'his countenance glowed'. It is also written that when Moses came down from Mt. Sinai with the second set of tablets of the Ten Commandments after 40 days and nights of being immersed in the presence of the Creator, his face was said to be so radiant, "as bright as the sun", that he had to don what was one of the first hoodies because people were afraid look directly at him.[50]

Halos above people's heads are another example of energetic phenomena. While probably not a perfect floating circle, a sort of energy vortex above their head is indicative of someone having opened that well-known energy center, called the 'crown' center. Although rare to fully achieve, people can see it, sense it and feel it.

The person who has accomplished this is often quite special and has access to much better 'in-waves' of elevated awareness.

However, there is one energy center that is easily the single most highly valued — and most shared — amongst all spiritual paths, all genuine religions and all true wisdom traditions. It is THE central energy center, similar to the nucleus of a cell, or the nucleus of an atom around which all the electrons gravitate, or like our sun around which all the planets of our solar system orbit.

Just as black holes are now shown to birth new stars,[51] this central energy center emits radiance. This is the ENERGY JOY engine in the center of your chest area. We can think of this as our 'Energy Heart'. It is as important and as central to our energy as our physical heart is to our life. Its radiance is the human form of the Energy of Life.

> **We experience this radiant out-wave as joy — because it is so valuable.**

Along with joy and generating the energy of life that creates and fuels your body, what other functions does it provide that make it so desirable?

Modern physics, using images from MRIs (magnetic resonance imaging) and S.Q.U.I.D. imaging (superconducting quantum interference device) have shown that there is a magnetic center of our human magnetic field in this exact central chest area. It radiates its field of energy out three feet or so around our entire body. Every cell, organ, gland and tissue bathes in this field and is permeated by it.

> **It is likely that this magnetic field is the medium whereby our 40-70 trillion cells can communicate with each other all at once all the time.**[52]

Nothing else in the body can handle such a level of signaling simultaneity. While our brain is super fast, its central nervous system operations are still sequential, not simultaneous. It cannot provide this foundational level of health because it is too linear, thus too slow and it doesn't go to every cell.

Given the fundamental primacy of signaling throughout the body for health and longevity, having our magnetic field strong, clean and free of blockages is the bottom line necessity for uplifting into new levels of optimal health.

> **Knowing how to nourish our magnetic field has become ever more important — and may soon be an absolute necessity — to stop cellphone tower microwaves from their harmful effects that distort, block and interfere with our body's healthy cellular signaling.**

Until we cease emitting the energy pollution of these toxic microwaves, 'diseases of miscommunication' like cancers, dementia and autoimmune problems will increase — because these microwaves permeate our buildings AND our bodies in their commercial quest for 'good reception' that increasingly intrudes into all areas of our life.

We also are exposed to invisible 'electrical pollution' which leaks out from wall sockets, insufficiently insulated electrical wires and ungrounded appliances.[53] Our health signals can be dangerously affected. Having a strong magnetic field is added protection.

Applying our wisdom tool: '*as above, so below; as within, so without*', illustrates the similar life-enhancing effects of the Earth's magnetic field. Geologists know that this magnetic field extends from the Earth's surface up about a mile into the atmosphere.[54]

While it is very weak, it seems to perfectly nourish biological life. It also provides the navigational guidance for the many migrating species, especially birds and butterflies that travel thousands of miles as well as salmon that return to their spawning ground roots. These species are known to have magnetite that somehow connects with the Earth's magnetic field for navigation. We humans also have magnetite in our brain.

> **For optimal health we require a coherent energy field that is strong and non-porous to everything unhealthy such as viruses, flu or other peoples' negativity.**

We want our energy field to function optimally — coherently — as a whole unit of accurate communication, from perceiving our external environment to accurately interpreting our internal sensations, emotions and bodily signals.

While books are written on this for people to read, the very best level of knowing comes from you directly experiencing the Energy of Life by turning on your own ENERGY JOY engine. It is one of the most delicious experiences we humans can have, as it fills us with the energy of joy and love.

How will this ability to feel and radiate joy change psychology, psychotherapy, marital relations and gatherings of people, when all can turn on their ENERGY JOY engine?

Moving our species out of the dominating emotions of survival — anger and fear — by establishing the emotions for uplifting — joy and love — marks the beginning of human ascension into our true potential, beyond any technological development. This is especially so because nearly all scientific and technological developments are still based on merely surviving. 'Market share' is but a subset of survival's quest for physical, emotional, attention and belief system domination.

> **I am saying — as directly as possible — that you have inside of your chest an ENERGY JOY engine which is an untapped source of the Energy of Life, whose flow you can open. It is the actual source at the energy level of our most prized emotions of joy and love.**

Why would joy and love be so enjoyable?

Joy and love are emotions that result from an increasing flow of the Energy of Life. Because we naturally want more, they entice us to find the 'valve' of the Energy of Life and open its flow more and more.

This means you can feel, have, enjoy and nourish yourself any time you wish with joy — which means you are opening and increasing the flow into you of the Energy of Life — just by turning on your ENERGY JOY engine.

This is a skill, so it takes experience to operate. But it gives you the most amazing uplift imaginable. And... the more you do it, the more potent it grows.

New super-healthy levels of cellular communication with enhanced signaling health from both external and internal environments are mighty motivations. When you add the anytime-you-want ability to feel joy and love by filling your body with a greater flow of the nourishing, uplifting Energy of Life, these two benefits should be enough to entice anyone into the quest to make your ENERGY JOY engine shine.

Yet many more fantastic abilities emerge with a healthy, coherent energy field filled with radiating your ENERGY JOY.

If scientists could measure this Energy of Life, they would discover that the more you understand about energy, the more highly valued ENERGY JOY is to you.* (See footnote below)

Let's explore why!

* This energy center in the center of our chest has been exalted from ancient times around the world and given many names by many cultural traditions. Western people today can recognize it from the Yogic spiritual paths of India, where it is called the 'heart chakra', and part of a central column of seven energy centers that are to be activated and inter-connected. In Judaism this energy center can be considered as 'teferet', the body's central energy radiance, described as 'beauty' and 'harmony' which successfully integrates kindness with discipline. It is part of the ten energy radiances called 'sefirot' which comprise the three columns of the 'Tree of Life'. Together these ten are considered the energetic blueprint of a human being. These energy radiances also are to be activated and inter-connected to form a coherent whole of energy that rejuvenates and elevates.

Your ENERGY JOY Engine

How to open the flow of the Energy of Life into your body.

---

1. **FEEL** the space that is the center of your chest inside your body. That is where you will find the 'flow valve' you want to relax open.
2. **PICTURE** a bright, shiny, radiant energy sphere in your chest center. SEE it as brilliant, vibrant golden/white/yellow light. FEEL it there.
3. **KEEP** your focus there, feeling AND seeing inside your chest.
4. **FEEL** where the 'flow valve' is inside of you. It is subtle, but you'll feel it. It is like a tight muscle in that space, which opens as you tell it to relax.
5. **FEEL** how to 'let go' more and more in that space inside your torso. Know that you are opening the flow valve and you'll feel it soon!
6. **SEE and FEEL** the bright golden/white/yellow light get brighter & brighter. Let its energy fill your entire body, as if your body is an empty shell and your ENERGY JOY engine is radiating liquid light. This is how you help heal and nourish your entire body and all its organs and cells, by infusing life energy into your physicality.
7. **ACTIVATE your ENERGY JOY** engine more fully by choosing to feel joy and love in the center of your chest, inside your energy sphere. You can do this by directly feeling joy and love, or you can generate joy or love by thinking of something that brings you joy, something you love. This can be a pet, a work of art, a special place in Nature, your favorite music, an activity you love – or whatever brings you joy. What you are doing is matching energy frequencies with the energy inside you that you want. This matching is like an energetic 'lock and key' that helps open the flow.
8. **FEEL** this joy and love inside the center of your energy sphere. Notice more and more precisely WHERE you feel the joy and love originate in your chest. That is where you'll find the 'flow valve'. FEEL what you are doing, like operating a tiny muscle, that opens the flow valve more and more. Everybody is unique, so you'll know because you'll feel some combination of increasing warmth, tingling, energy and joy.
9. **STREAMLINE** your focus so you can quickly, easily and precisely FEEL how you open your flow valve and feel ENERGY JOY whenever you want. This may take several practice sessions. But once you locate your flow valve and feel how to relax it open, you can feel joy immediately at will. You can also feel how to grow more and more ENERGY JOY.

This is the treasure! Keep at it until you find your 'valve'. Your body will love you!

29

WHAT YOUR ENERGY JOY ENGINE SHINES

As a hybrid of physical and non-physical, we are like a new species of physical beings who can also bear non-physical fruit.[55] What we can do is completely phenomenal and magnificent in the very best of ways. We are like the bumble bees and pollinators of the insect world, except that we are pollinating the fabric of physical reality itself.

With our ENERGY JOY engine turned on, we are opening the flow of the human form of the Energy of Life into physicality and into the biosphere of our Earth Mother. This is the gift our human species can contribute to our Earth Mother and to all her life forms. While every living being has their own connection with this energy, or they wouldn't exist, we as humans can uniquely bring this elixir of life in abundance, uplifting all life on Earth into a new era.

> **This is what elevates our species out of survival. We bear fruit delicious to life.**

From the Dalai Lama's book, we have this fascinating report.

> *"A scientifically controlled study conducted by German researchers at the University of Kassel has shown that while the chest area of an average person emits only 20 photons of light per second, someone who meditates on their heart center and sends love and light to others emits an amazing 100,000 photons per second. That is 5000 times more than the average human being. Numerous studies have also shown that* ***when these photons are infused with a loving and healing intent, their frequency and vibration increase to the point where they can literally change matter, heal disease, and transform negative events."*** [56]

Imagine yourself having the ability to change matter, heal disease and transform negative events with your ENERGY JOY engine! This is our potential.

The Dalai Lama comments that even ten minutes of meditating in this way will give you a calm and joyous mind all day! Meditating on concepts like compassion and kindness are truly wonderful and effective. Yet they are indirect ways of activating our ENERGY JOY engine. For even greater benefits, we can directly energize.

Keeping in mind that our DNA stores its information in photons of light, what 'information' might be emitted from a radiant ENERGY JOY engine?

> **The Energy of Life delivers the equivalent of a much higher level DNA that grows life itself — with new levels of health, vitality, awareness, joy, peacefulness, consciousness, wisdom, understanding and collaboration.**

This is the ultimate 'fix-it' energy spray for life on Earth. While it is challenging to comprehend its enormity, the 'content' that the

Energy of Life delivers is exponentially more coherent. **ENERGY JOY delivers awareness from the living Mind of the source of the Energy of Life.**

ENERGY JOY opens this flow, like a pipeline, for us to enjoy a more direct, personal and vitalizing connection to what can be thought of as the Source of Life. Achieving this opening of energy flow is the ultimate goal of all genuine spiritual paths, all wisdom traditions and all true religions.

> **All the effective meditative type tools and functional religious practices are designed to open this flow of the Energy of Life — to eventually gain access to that Mind.**

Individuals throughout history have traveled far and wide to gain this knowledge. Now it is time for our entire human species to blossom this fruit of ours by fully turning on our ENERGY JOY engines!

With our ENERGY JOY engine on, we can establish a conduit of communication for an entirely unique two-way energy exchange whereby:

1. We tune into and receive the life-nourishing instructions we call guidance, intuition, creativity and innovation for growing better, healthier and more joyous life on Earth

2. We also can send out our best intentions and increasingly receive them back as 'blossoms' we grow in our physical reality.

Is it that easy? Why wouldn't everybody be doing it already?

Why does your ENERGY JOY engine not turn on and emit its uplifting joy from the very first time you try to activate it? What prevents your ENERGY JOY engine from shining?

In a way, the ENERGY JOY engine reflects your relationship with your Self. Some people can visualize it all the way through the exercise, but do not feel it. Sometimes people fall asleep when focusing inward with their eyes closed for more than a few minutes.

There is a 'zone' that you can become very comfortable and familiar with, so that you can hang out in it as long as you want. This zone is more quiet than normal awake type awareness, but you are definitely not asleep. In fact, you can become far more aware than normal 'awake'. Experienced meditators, creative people and artists cultivate this zone because it develops their awareness so remarkably. More subtle communications like the famous 'small, quiet voice within' can then be better heard, and visual images can be seen with greater clarity.

Cultivating your Dynamic Calm zone is hugely rewarding, because it also enhances your perception of energy. Your five senses expand their operating from exclusively physical realm events into more 'invisible' awareness. Practically speaking, this more refined awareness enables your creativity, intuition, innovation and inner guidance for solutions to be enhanced enormously. The secret is to be more fully 'present' to what you ARE perceiving rather than what you are not perceiving.

But there is a larger obstacle.

We can think of our ENERGY JOY engine as the equivalent of our heart, but at the energy level. Just like fat deposits can clog our blood vessels, there is often a type of shell containing your 'Energy Heart' and restricting it from beaming brightly.* (See footnote below)

Like an energy prison, this shell is an organized structure made of the conclusions about life and the beliefs about yourself that you have accepted from the experiences that your traumas, disappointments, hurts, sorrows, fears, anxieties, failures and limitations others have imposed upon you.

None of these are the real you. Like the buildup of a plaque formation in our blood, our 'negativity' accumulates as energy that forms this energy blocking shell.

Remember: everything is energy. The energy shell around your 'Energy Heart' needs to be removed. Successful psychotherapy can sometimes dissolve it entirely, but mostly chips away at it, as evidenced by many issues requiring years of therapy sessions. The aim is to resolve the emotional and psychological levels of the traumas and to debunk their limiting beliefs, replacing them with more relevant, useful and accurate beliefs. But until the energy level structures holding those events in place are dissolved, they can still reappear and cause upsets.

---

* In the Torah, *the Five Books of Moses,* (Deuteronomy 10:16), Moses tells the Jewish people that they need to "cut away the barrier of your heart and no longer stiffen your neck." The Sages comment that: *"It is as if the heart is surrounded by a covering that dulls their spiritual perception."*

Again (Deuteronomy 30:6) Moses tells Israel that the Creator "shall circumcise your heart and the heart of your offspring, enabling you to love your G-d, with all your heart and with all your souls, so that you may live." The Sages comment that this means: *"removing spiritual impediments, and further, that this barrier prevents goodness from dominating the heart, so its circumcision removes from humanity the natural desire to sin."* The 18th century Sage, Rabbi Shneur Zalman of Lyady, comments that: *"This will liberate your Godly spark, enabling it to express itself freely throughout your entire being."*

Exactly.

Sometimes the traumas making the shell won't dissolve easily. This indicates their function is to remain until the messages of the traumas are identified, respected and acted upon to correct course. This is therapy success.

> **Fortunately, the ENERGY JOY engine directly dissolves that energy shell at the energy level.**

You accomplish this Einstein way of healing in two main ways. First, you continue energizing your ENERGY JOY engine more and more each day with a short focusing effort of four minutes or longer.

Second, a zillion times each day, you simply remember you now have an Energy Heart.

You don't need to go through the entire sequence. For a nano-second, you just picture and feel your Energy Heart shining brightly in the center of your chest and radiate out its ENERGY JOY. Done!

> **What you are doing is training yourself to turn on your ENERGY JOY engine instantly and powerfully.**

Each time you do this, you are also weakening and dissolving the shell from the inside. At some point, you'll blast through that shell, and you will feel a delicious burst of ENERGY JOY! Soon, with more effort, you will dissolve the entire shell around your Energy Heart, so your joy energy can flow fully and freely.

That is the goal!

Feeling joy whenever you want is such an amazing treasure that it is very much worth your efforts to turn on your ENERGY JOY engine. Your ability to grow joy only increases!

Once your ENERGY JOY engine is purring, a wondrous new world of energy opens up for you.

30

THE MIND OF THE ENERGY OF LIFE

A fascinating focus is to ponder what could be the creating source of the Energy of Life.

While some people might prefer 'random' to be an answer, that stops all exploration of knowledge and eliminates all the fun. Plus, the chance of life being random doesn't exist in reality. It's altogether too multi-dimensionally amazing. Saying it is random merely describes the currently limited awareness of our mind to fathom beyond the lock our five senses have on the physical material plane.

Having such a paucity of 'in-waves' can be greatly remedied with ENERGY JOY.

We know that 'everything is energy'. This is almost true. Everything is indeed energy — except for one thing.

What could that be?

Energy.

Energy itself is not entirely energy. It has content. Among its many functions, energy is a delivery system for this content. What content does the Energy of Life deliver?

Fortunately, we can utilize our wisdom tool *'as above, so below; as within, so without'*.

While our cellular DNA has its information for growth and repair stored in photons of light, and sunlight has its special ingredients for activating biological life, the Energy of Life carries far more intriguing content. Its content is somehow able to grow life itself and direct itself into life's enormous variety of forms.

Without the Energy of Life, we and all other living creatures would simply not exist. It has such fluidity, power and constant presence that you would think it is itself alive.

And so it is.

> **The content of the Energy of Life is a living awareness, the very consciousness of 'being' alive.**

This essence of life is the fruit blossomed into all living things. Each living thing has its own unique level of this living awareness, tailored to its purpose. Yet the Energy of Life is itself not fragmented nor separated from its source, even when its local purpose is limited.

We can usefully think of this awareness as 'The Mind' of the Energy of Life. This 'Mind' is continuously creating, growing and directing all living things. It is as high and deep as you can imagine, yet far more so.

> *"As a man who has devoted his whole life to the most clear-headed science, to the study of matter, I can tell you as a result of my research about atoms this much: There is no matter as such. All matter originates and exists only by virtue of a force which brings the particle of an atom to vibration and holds this most minute solar system of the atom together. We must assume behind this force the existence of a conscious and intelligent mind. This mind is the matrix of all matter."*
>
> — Max Planck, Physicist

Our human body is designed to produce this Energy of Life!

By activating and turning on your ENERGY JOY engine, you are opening a sort of energy gateway — a kind of flow valve — from the source of the Energy of Life. In many religions and spiritual traditions, this is likely what is poetically referred to as 'the Divine spark' and even 'the Kingdom of Heaven within'.

In most people it is indeed a tiny spark, emitting only a pinhole of light, because their ENERGY JOY engine is not turned on. Their Energy of Life valve is mostly closed and shut down, not open and flowing.

Stress, depression, despair, anger, fear and other 'negative' experiences are sure indications that the Energy of Life valve is not open. As a clue to energy health, our focusing on things we want LESS OF also closes the Energy of Life valve.

That lack of flow is a huge part of why we don't feel good. It's our signal to open the flow. Often, when we simply re-open this energy valve, we can feel better immediately, even while the reason we felt bad is not eliminated. We're clearly designed to flourish by having that open. Too many people are missing out on their treasure.

Your ENERGY JOY engine radiates this Energy of Life — which we feel as joy — into your body, your field and into the living energy matrix, the quantum field of our Earth Mother.

Most incredibly, this Energy of Life delivers 'The Mind' into the living energy fabric of our entire biosphere. This is what we are here to do as individuals and as a species.

Is that a good thing?

The very best. This 'Mind' only wants to create and blossom the very healthiest and most joyous life possible. This 'Mind' wants total prosperity at all levels. This 'Mind' creates life. So it knows. We only have to welcome it in.

A far greater whole is yet to be completed. This is 'The Uplift'.

Merely surviving on Earth is not the end goal. It was just a phase to accomplish — which stabilizes human life — so that we can keep moving up. Physicists call this advancement 'non-equilibrium phase transitions to macroscopic order'.[57] This is simply evolving into a greater whole — into new, more stable dynamic levels of organization.

Where can we move up to?

This is also built into our species' DNA. Four more growth stages await us humans.

It's time for the grand reveal.

PART V:

OUR BIGGEST WIN

We the People of the Earth
need to simply agree on
one highest value that we all
honor all the time.

31

UPLIFTING

Our Four Amazing Stages

As our species awakens to a far better reality beyond mere survival, by choosing to live the values which actually nourish life, we become aware of the path laid out before us from very ancient times.

For millennia, every culture and tradition throughout the world have included in their teachings some form of four very intriguing phrases.

Surviving by appearing in the guise of poetry and impossibly delightful fantasies, these phrases are actually precise goals for humanity to strive toward. As our species level DNA, they have always been our guidance — seeds planted in our human psyche to sprout when the time is ripe.

Centuries of struggling with the rotten fruit of a survival-based value system have now given us all the proof we need to openly welcome a genuine roadmap to real prosperity that we can actually enjoy, beyond the theoretical promises of any 'ism'.

The energetic blueprint that directs the growth of every living thing — each according to its purpose and function — has well established itself in our species as a whole. It illuminates the blossoming of our human contributions to biological life which will be what makes us exceedingly valuable to all the living creatures of the biosphere, and to our Earth Mother's beautiful being.

These contributions, the first one in particular, will ensure our survival.

STAGE ONE UPLIFTING: Peace on Earth

Our next stage of human development has been called: 'Peace on Earth'. This is the foundation for all subsequent advancement of our species' existence. Without Peace on Earth, we remain in the increasingly destructive death spiral which mere survival perpetuates.

Imagine the benefits of authentic, genuine peace all over the Earth — peace that everybody can trust and count on, no matter where we go and with whom we engage.

Once we agree to honor the Prime Directive to nourish life, and we begin to re-purpose all our efforts, activities, sciences, education and global economic reward systems to further the two essential values of health and joy, then Peace on Earth naturally blossoms.

We no longer need war, or pollution, nor enslaving people to work for ventures that do not nourish life. We never did. Only a few hyperactive control freaks throughout history, — overly endowed with narcissistic cruelty, hatred, bigotry, greed, deceit, anger and fear — were able to force or entice others to do their dirty work. There is no honor in that.

Sane humans, like all creatures on Earth, just want to live in peace and enjoy their lives. 'Turning swords into plow sheds' is wise guidance.

Invoking our wisdom tool *'as above, so below; as within, so without'*, we can easily see that when a body has 'peace' that body thrives, because it is not using all its energy battling infections, illness, disease, stress and despair. Its life energy goes to healing, nourishing, growing, uplifting, strengthening, fueling and enjoying its real desires and goals. Doctors prescribe 'rest' to achieve this exact result.

As individuals we can achieve this inner peace easily with the skills of Dynamic Calm.

An ecological system gains similar benefits when its community of living creatures do not have to deal with battling pollution and contamination of its elements – air, water, soil, electromagnetic field. That ecosystem then thrives and generates abundance of healthy life. Every part of the natural world that is free of damaging human footprints sports exuberant and magnificent energies of life. Our national parks, forests, rainforests and wildernesses have this treasured existence.

Why not all of the Earth?

While this might seem a wishful fantasy from the handicap of our current survival–imprisoned mentality, it is nonetheless true. Nourishing biological life into increasing ecological prosperity that benefits all other life is simply biological intelligence. We humans need to step up into reality. Author Paul Hawken describes how this is immanently doable in his book: *Regeneration: Ending the Climate Crisis in One Generation*.[58]

Darwin explored how the present developed from the past. We must now explore how we use the present to develop the future we want and value.

STAGE TWO UPLIFTING: The Golden Age of Humanity

When we are solidly living Peace on Earth — with our energies, resources and creativity all directed to nourishing life — an abundance of new inventions, ideas, products, goods and services will blossom into the consciousness of people worldwide. Those who develop their ability to tune into our Earth Mother and the Mind of the Energy of Life, by accessing their intuition as the content delivered with ENERGY JOY, will be the first to 'get' these inspirations for a new world.

And they will be well rewarded by the new, functional economic system that values health and joy.

Imagine decades of progress from all humans focused on nourishing life in over seven billion unique, creative and innovative ways! This will usher in a true golden age. All wisdom traditions and genuine religions around the world have predicted this. It is in our species' energetic blueprint to achieve. We only need to choose it.

STAGE THREE UPLIFTING: Heaven on Earth

It is a crazy endeavor to conceptualize 'Heaven on Earth'. Yet this is exactly what we are to use our focus to 'ask and receive', like an African 'call and response' from the Mind of the Energy of Life. It already knows.

Taking advantage of how the living energy matrix of our Earth Mother's quantum field operates, we tune our focus to direct content in the two-way communication that tells this Mind that we want the ultimate and most amazing reality possible here on Earth.

The more we do, the more we receive.

It's a process that will continually inspire, delight and fascinate us. Who could ask for more than the joy of ushering in a reality so wondrous, joyous and phenomenal that it is deemed 'Heaven on Earth'?

STAGE FOUR UPLIFTING: The Garden of Eden

Again, translating from the original Hebrew in the Torah, 'Gan Eden' literally means 'Garden of Delights'. What could this be, if not fantastical beyond our current capacity to even imagine?

This refers in some way to a very highly evolved human species who has learned how to focus in ways that direct energy and deliver content which manifests physically rather rapidly if not immediately. We shall have become expert operators of our quantum reality.

This ability is also deeply embedded in our human psyche with the phrase 'abra k'dabra'. What is that? As ancient Hebrew, it literally means "it appears as I speak". This alludes to a kind of power to directly influence reality to grant one's wishes, to manifest and to create something from nothing.

Ancient Hebrew is said to be the 'Holy Tongue' which had this capability. Biblically, that capability was also said to have been removed at the occasion of the Tower of Babel, when people got together to misuse it for nefarious purposes – the usual attempts to control the Earth.

While not everyone speaking Hebrew could make miracles, there are many, many stories of people who could and did. Several other traditions around the world have their own stories and versions of ancient language that affects reality, as well as ceremonies and rituals which 'do things'. Blessings, prayers, ceremonies and healings are modern versions, which sometimes work and sometimes do not.

However, the original knowledge was often described as a science.

Where did it go? How do we bring it back?

Wisdom traditions understand why that level of influence has been denied to humanity for millennia – because we are too raw and un-evolved to do anything but generate constant survival-based destruction and tyranny with such power. Giving the power to manifest thoughts into reality to people who have not outgrown their survival values to dominate, control, destroy and enslave is like handing a nuclear bomb to a child.

Learning by analogy from the Biblical description of expulsion from Gan Eden, our abilities to enjoy this wondrous paradise of physical reality have been dumbed down by not honoring the abundance already given and by trying to take more than was given.

Highly spiritual people today can often direct energy to accomplish results – like healings and blessings. The best of these people have earned their abilities because they know to use it only for good.

There are indeed people today who can 'do things'. The wisest only do that which serves Life, not their personal agendas. The lesser players may have some capabilities, but they can never escape the dire consequences of misusing that knowledge. It will bite them hard at very inconvenient times totally out of their control. That's 'The Law'.

These rules are basic to energetic level alignment. If your frequency or 'vibration' is at a low level – stuck in survival – you simply cannot match the higher frequencies of energy that communicate effectively to the quantum field. You cannot enter the realms where the focused intentions we call wishes and blessings are easily 'granted'.

Our species has quite a journey before we can uplift into the level of the Garden of Delights. Yet, it is our direction and our possible destiny. The key is how we use our free will – our intentions as the content of the energy that our focus directs into the quantum field.

Once we begin, we shall progress.

We shall be met and welcomed more than halfway.

By what?

32

REALITY

The Being

No human mind can fully grasp, comprehend or even fathom the enormous totality of 'being'. Existence has been the subject of countless philosophies, with its nature and purpose likely speculated upon from the night before the dawn of humanity.

'Being' includes everything — the entire known universe of stars, planets, black holes, space, time, life, afterlife, soul, awareness and humor. Except for retelling bad jokes, all of 'being' is dynamic. It is all alive, vibrant and changing, yet somehow continuous without interruption.

Let's leap up to consider the very greatest whole, the whole of which all other wholes are but parts.

What is this?

Reality itself is a living being.

Doesn't it seem alive? While we usually think of aliveness in terms of physical creatures like animals, birds, plants, insects and some people, Reality also meets all of our qualities for being alive. It has a stable core structure but is somewhat fluid. It responds to our thoughts, actions and intentions. It changes and grows. Everything within it moves, lives, dies and is replaced with new forms.

Why wouldn't the entire universe be a single gigantic living being? How could it not be?

Its galaxy clusters look just like nerve pathways in our brain. Why would they not be functioning in a similar but far grander, more universal manner? It's like the question: "If a tree falls in a forest, does it make any noise if nobody is there to hear it"? Just because we humans don't know what the galaxies might be saying to each other doesn't mean they are not busily chatting.

The stars could easily be akin to the energy centers in our bodies. Stars have a life cycle like all living things. Black holes seem like pores in our skin or orifices where things go in and in some cases newly born stars are excreted.[59]

Certainly seems quite alive!

While we don't yet know what's on the other end of a black hole, it is likely an inner realm of 'being' of which the physical universe is but the outer and perhaps even the smaller part — like a single leaf on a tree. And that inner realm might itself have a yet larger environment of some nature. Beyond that it may go on and on.

That is exactly how ancient knowledge describes our physical universe, as being the lowest of four far grander universes from which our reality is formed and constantly maintained.

Yet it is all connected as a single 'being'. No part of it can be disconnected from the whole and still 'be'.

The BEING that is Reality is the only 'Being' there is.

The entirety of this 'BEING', mightily magnificent, far exceeds our ability to comprehend.

Fortunately, it's not our job to figure it all out.

One thing we can conclude is that 'It' seems to know what 'It' is doing. A second thing we can recognize is that the inner realm of our physical universe, and certainly everything beyond that, is not limited to 'the physical'. We simply do not know what its nature may be. Nor do we need to know. We're here to open the flow and enjoy life.

Our scientists have surmised that from the assumed beginning of our known universe — through the formation of stars, planets, our solar system, planet Earth and biological life that now includes humans — it has been around 13 billion years in the making, give or take a few seconds.

Again, with the help of our wisdom tool *'as above, so below; as within, so without'*, we can envision this entire creation as being like an agricultural harvest born from planting seeds earlier in very carefully prepared soil, and tending to it throughout its entire gestation.

What is the crop being grown?

The harvest that we can perceive and experience is what we call our reality. Imagine growing something that takes 13 billion years! For all we know, to the BEING that is Reality, this entire universe might be the equivalent of the fingernail on our little finger.

Perspective.

We, and all life on Earth, are like blossoming fruit growing more of this all-encompassing BEING into physicality. We are growing Life!

Of course, people, religions, spiritual teachings and wisdom traditions have their names for this 'BEING'. We come to love these names because we associate them with the source and gardener of this amazing adventure called life. These names also serve to streamline our focus. As representations they help stabilize our contact with this BEING.

Even so, however glorious, honored and esteemed, the names are not the entire BEING itself. How could they be? Nor can an image, statue or any human-made object, however well-intentioned and beautifully crafted, fully represent this BEING that is all of reality itself.

Yet, we want and seek ways to connect more directly.

When we pray, ask for guidance, seek blessings or request healing, protection, love, success, solutions, assistance or being 'saved', this is the BEING we aim our focused energy towards. How is it that we humans all over the world since our species' beginning seem to all share this experience?

> **We innately know that there is something 'there' that listens and can respond.**

We communicate with that BEING through our heartfelt intentions, our speech and by demonstrating our sincerity through actions such as meditating, vision quests, fasting, disciplines, gratitude, ceremonies, rituals and honoring special times of the year.

And we know through millennia of experience that sometimes... it works!

Kind of amazing. And intriguing.

There seems to be a 'MIND' of multi-universe proportions that is always aware of our personal needs, wants and desires. In retrospect, when we reflect on the events in our lives, we often have to conclude that we were also 'guided' quite exquisitely to get where we are.

What might such a BEING want from us?

Are we created into being and given life for no reason? Or is it perhaps just for amusement of this BEING? Is it possibly to accomplish something important?

Those people stuck in survival would likely opt for 'no reason'. Existentialists and cynics might select 'for amusement'. Hence, humor.

But if the latter, what?

Like living the ultimate detective game, we could say there are clues.

33

THE CLUES

Life itself is interactive at all levels. Not just some, but all levels. Connecting the dots of reality reveals an entire set of clues for human success as a species, like a yellow brick road to the Emerald City. These clues include what not to do as well.

Once you realize that the entirety of 'Reality' is an alive and conscious BEING, you can start to recognize that you — and all of us — are being communicated with continuously. The adventure now is how to understand the content of the communications and how to respond appropriately. It seems likely that our human evolutionary journey has been to arrive at this point.

Why in the world do joy and love feel so good? They didn't have to.

Evolutionarily, they clearly motivate, inspire and entice us to want more. But why?

Why does health at all levels feel good and enable us to live more fully?

Why would stress, anxiety, heart disease, cancers and all illnesses feel so terrible and be so debilitating?

Why do depression, hatred, cruelty and other expressions of survival's dominant emotions of anger and fear feel horrible and cause such destructiveness?

These are very blatant guidance system communications — for life — of basic good versus bad, right versus wrong, true versus false. We want MORE OF the good stuff and LESS OF the harmful stuff. So we begin focusing our attention to figure out what works in each direction.

> **Limited to a survival mentality, we have settled for mediocrity.**

Fortunately, we also have people of genuine wisdom amongst us who see clearly and can interpret what the Mind of the Energy of Life is communicating to us. But not everyone can 'hear' what these exceptional humans have to say. Nor can most people discern who is speaking truth and who is not, especially if their message is 'different' or is not what they want to hear.

These capabilities are dependent upon what wisdom traditions call our 'personal power'.

A survival era mentality imagines 'power' to be about might, force, control, strength and lethal capabilities. But when we enter the wave of uplifting, real 'power' is awareness. The power of our awareness to tune into and accurately interpret communications from the Mind of the Energy of Life gives us special advantages.

We start by reading the signs from our Earth Mother, now more important than ever as we are forced to navigate powerfully destructive global weather events. Politicians, corporate executives, money managers, media personalities and many people triumphant in the current status quo — with a mentality built upon centuries of survival and industrial strength ambitions — may be the last to want to even hear that change is needed. Their motivation to change can be weak or non-existent. If they are 'values diseased', they can be motivated to resist and thwart needed change, no matter how obviously beneficial and necessary to the rest of life.

People may call that 'human nature', but it is quite contrary to the real Nature of healthy biological reality — our Earth Mother's biosphere. The key to every species survival, that which insures successful adapting to change, is mutually beneficial collaboration.

How does Nature communicate? Her 'opportunity awareness signals' are not in words.

> *"We are facing a dangerous period ahead. If we do not stop, correct and change some of these wrongdoings, now, we are all going to suffer. Either things we make will overtake us or nature will take over. Earthquakes, floods, rain, severe drought, severe winter, lightning destruction, great wind destruction...these things will warn us that we're not following the law of the Great Spirit."*
>
> —Thomas Banyacya, Hopi, Sept. 5, 2017

So... why would 'the best' of our human experiences be filled with love and joy?

It's because joy IS our guidance.

Joy and love are most fascinating because they eventually bring our attention to where we feel them originate in our body. We are led to the center of our chest. As we grow our awareness, we can feel where the energy 'valve' is in our chest. Then we feel how to open it.

What happens?

We get a delicious blast of the Energy of Life, which energizes us with even more joy and love to reward us for having focused there. With experience, our ENERGY JOY engine activates. It also delivers a subtle uplifting increase in awareness, understanding and healthy coherence. The communications have a delivery vehicle.

Or... by just pursuing joy and love in our lives, we keep opening that flow and nourishing ourselves with more of the Energy of Life. Either way, we are being trained to seek — and guided interactively to find — what is most valuable in life.

We learn how to turn on our Energy Heart!

The clues of mutually beneficial collaboration are found in abundance.

Into our lungs we breathe oxygenated air provided by the plants of our environment while exhaling our waste gas of carbon dioxide, which plants utilize. Once in our lungs, oxygen journeys into our blood, which then delivers this primary fuel into our tissues and cells where countless tinier interactive energy exchanges take place.

Plants use energy from the sun to convert carbon dioxide from the air along with water and minerals from the soil into carbohydrates and other molecules that form our food — roots, stems, leaves, seeds, vegetables and fruits — and all our needed medicines.

Plants keep us and all CO2-emitting creatures alive, which further ensures their survival as plants. Collaboration uplifts. Plants are indispensable for biological life. Destroying forests and the rain forests by idolatrous Enemies of Life threatens millions of years of fruitful collaboration, more than we know.

At a different level of interactivity, matter is made from energy and then matter is metabolized back into energy that fuels life's processes.

Many indigenous peoples consider the elements of air, water, earth and fire as each a sort of 'being' that is alive in its own way. Amongst indigenous traditions is the knowledge to interact with these elements and even direct them to some extent.

As a 'being', air gives us the essential content of our every breath — which we absolutely need for life. It has made itself into THE single most essential element, providing the foundation for all biological life. So... its gift is priceless, irreplaceable, and cherished. In return, all biological life accepts air as a sort of top 'brand' and as the agreed-upon standard for running our biological machinery.

There are also people who talk to water as a 'being'. And... it responds to their requests. What would Earth life be without water?

Can we humans be as indispensable?

A major clue is that in the fullness of interactivity throughout the entire biosphere, healthy ecosystems have no waste. One species' out-wave is another species' nourishing in-wave. The healthy exchange of energy and information is everywhere.

This is a concept called 'coupling' in science. Just like hydrogen atoms couple with oxygen to form water, humans need to couple with the biosphere in only health-producing ways. As mentioned, our current economic reward system is de-coupled from biological reality, which has allowed human activities to spew waste too toxic for any other species to survive around, much less to use, and which can take millennia to biodegrade if at all.

Healthy functioning in living systems can be thought of as degrees of 'coherence' or wholeness. For example, malignant tumors are considered cells that have become permanently de-coupled from their whole. They no longer receive nor respond to health signals from the organism they were part of. Decay, entropy and tissue death result.

Being connected to its greater whole is essential for all parts of any living system.

In bio-physics, a living system can be considered as one coherent 'photon field' bound to living matter. This photon field is fully coupled internally, such that any energy input will be fully and quickly delocalized throughout all the frequencies of the whole field.[58] This means all the photons of light in a living system are connected to each other and together form a field of interacting photons — a 'quantum' field of energy as light.

When we consider that health signaling circulates its nourishing information optimally and simultaneously through our electro-magnetic field, our energy skin, all parts must be included for optimal health.

If we again invoke our wisdom tool, *"as above, so below; as within, so without"*, it would make sense that there also are larger energy fields that we are naturally within and interacting with, like that of our Earth Mother.

It is time we consciously couple 'up'.

Why wouldn't the process of interactivity for mutual benefit also exist between our human species and the living energy matrix of our Earth Mother, and with its even greater whole: the BEING that is Reality?

While all of life interacts in mutually beneficial ways, the BEING that is Reality has also brilliantly created direct communication to and from 'It'. Two-way means more than us only asking for favors. We thrive by learning to behave in ways that are mutually beneficial, because... these are the ways that best nourish life.

As we uplift our comprehension of our physical world to include the more impactful and essential operation of things at the energy level, we can begin to 'see' with wisdom.

> **Certain energies open the flow of the treasured Energy of Life — which delivers nourishment plus communication from and to the BEING. Other energies close the gates. And some energies slam the gates shut and lock them forever.**

Keeping in mind that 'everything is energy', this means our thoughts, feelings, intentions, speech and actions are all forms of energy as well. Because the interactive quantum field somehow 'hears' these as our energy out-waves, they become our communications to the BEING that is Reality.

While our output as an individual may not be super potent, as a species we are always 'broadcasting' into the living energy matrix of our Earth Mother with our predominant thoughts. This living energy matrix is a subset, our local part of the BEING that is the entirety of Reality.

> **Given that this BEING is the source of all life AND can choose to grant all our wishes, we might want to figure out how to best cultivate our connection and communications with 'It'.**

A good relationship could be our most rewarding investment.

Removing obstructions, tuning into 'It' and opening the flow of its Energy of Life are the keys to our uplifting. This is why all religious, spiritual and wisdom traditions teach some form of ethics and morality. These qualities — and those like kindness, generosity and compassion — function energetically to keep our energy field clean of energy level debris and to keep our field in the higher frequency ballpark of resonating with the Energy of Life — so that we can be 'in touch'. These ethics are not simply goodie-goodie niceties, but work as highly purposeful energy flow operations.

> **The prize is receiving and interacting with the content the Energy of Life delivers.**

The Energy of Life elevates and informs our consciousness with brilliant and creative solutions to our challenges as guidance to navigate the events we encounter. The Energy of Life also establishes health with its greater coherence, as it aligns us with itself, which is the source of life. It's not polluted, contaminated, distorted nor malevolent in any way. The Energy of Life is pure. Like fresh clean, pristine water, it washes away illness of body, mind, energy and spirit.

How do we uplift our frequencies, our 'vibrations' and the quality of energy we resonate?

The direct way we accelerate or 'raise' our frequencies is by strengthening, growing and blossoming our Energy Heart. The more brightly we radiate its ENERGY JOY, the more fully this Energy of Life fills our body and our energetic field around us. And... the more it permeates our physical being, the more fully we can perceive what's inside this energy — the living awareness of the Mind of the Energy of Life.

As a species and as individuals, we are in the quest to grow our coherence — to become healthier, better functioning parts of a greater whole.

Because energy delivers information, each level of energetic frequencies delivers its corresponding level of content — and awareness.

To expand our species' focus out of survival and into the more elevated frequencies of uplifting, we radiate ENERGY JOY into our body and into our energy field. Doing this is made easier by aligning our four major body systems into their respective treasure modes using Dynamic Calm. We can then better apply the Genius Focus to communicate what we want MORE OF to our Earth Mother, and simultaneously to the BEING that is Reality (as different levels of the awareness spectrum).

Remember: your HPA-axis is your tuner!

With this combo, our 'opportunity awareness signals' expand their range of operation into those of uplifting from the restrictive survival level perceptions. We upgrade.

Increasingly, we receive the guidance and intuition for how to manifest effectively — both what we want MORE OF and what our Earth Mother wants — into reality.

What is the goal?

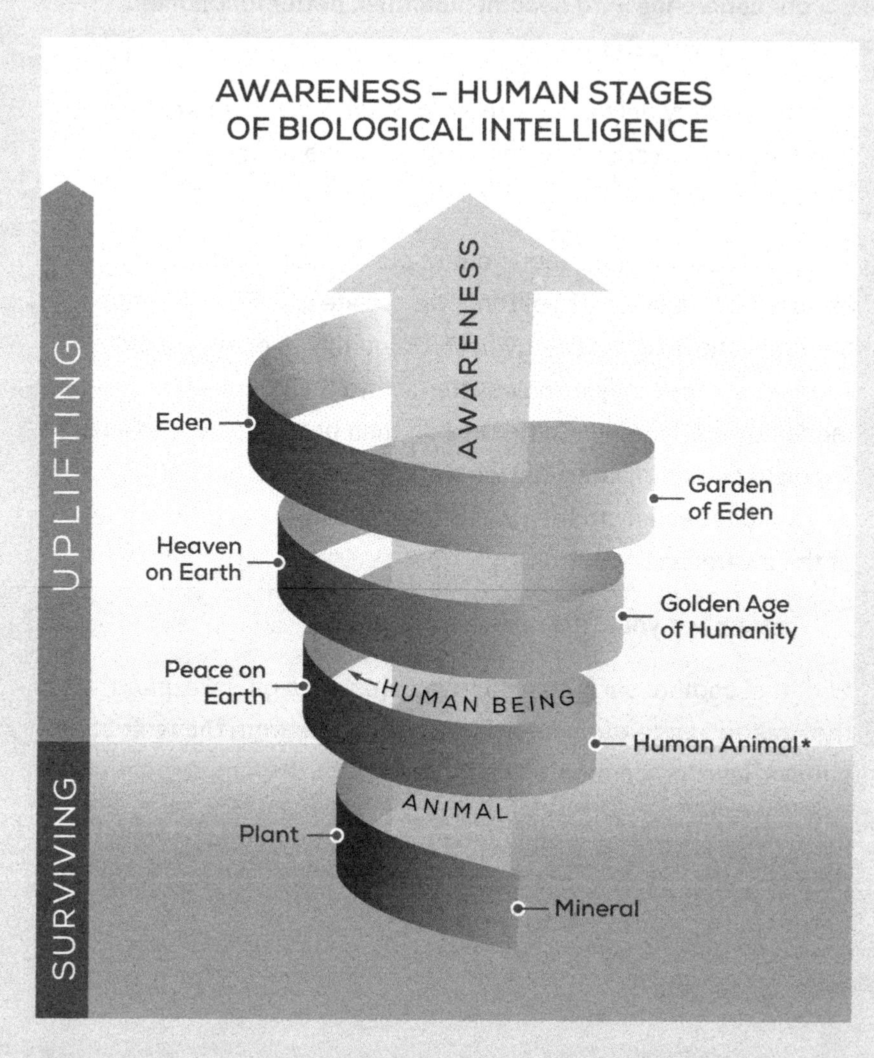

**We are HERE at a most momentous, epoch-making and consequential precipice of applying our species' knowledge to either uplift into 'Peace on Earth' and become real human beings or slide backwards into devastating basic survival.*

Awareness

Human Stages of Biological Intelligence

Humans still living in a survival value system of 'us against them' are only human animals.

Our industrial progress and technological sophistication, used to acquire survival values of power and control, are contaminating Earth's biological resources, making us 'Enemies of Life'.

We become real human beings by collaborating with biological reality as a species, so we are contributing to the healthy prosperity of the entire biosphere. We have yet to experience the phenomenal benefits of committing to this journey of uplifting together, but ancient traditions around the world allude to four more advanced, joyous and delightfully intriguing stages of uplifting inherent in our species' DNA.

Continually raising our awareness is our evolutionary vehicle because it gives us better access to these original instructions for growing healthiest life. So superior are these innate instructions to anything people can invent, that they are called: 'Divine Will'. The Energy of Life delivers them with ENERGY JOY. Our biological intelligence grows by discovering how to nourish things so they flourish best, making us 'Lovers of Life'.

All spiritual/religious/wisdom traditions teach individuals to dismantle their 'ego' in order to tune into and receive these valuable gifts of 'spirit'. Likewise, it is by dismantling the ego arrogance of our species that we gain access – not by manipulating biology to exert dominance. Our ultimate goal is to increasingly connect with the 'MIND' or consciousness of the BEING that is reality itself. This is how we fulfill our species' purpose: bringing into physicality something so superlative that it is called 'the Divine'.

34

ECO-JOY

Biosphere Gold

Everything is energy, including you. This means at your essence, you are a kind of energy being.

As a living being, as 'a coherent photon field of light bound to matter', we want to activate our human body by turning on the ancient allusion to this dormant but essential part of us, which has been poetically called the 'light within', the 'divine spark', the gateway to the 'kingdom of Heaven within' and other descriptions.

This is your Energy Heart. It grows you into your Big Mind — with energy. It communicates to all of life that that you are radiating ENERGY JOY.

Because this ENERGY JOY is so nourishing to life, biological life loves you. Imagine being loved by trees, birds, animals and even rocks. When you beam them in ENERGY JOY, which they immediately feel, they send back ENERGY JOY to you. With practice of 'tuning', you can definitely feel their energy.

You become lovers, energy lovers.

What is incredibly fascinating is that their ENERGY JOY also contains and delivers to you the content which is their thoughts, feelings and intentions. So as you learn to open your Energy Heart more and more, and its Energy of Life more fully permeates your electromagnetic field and your physical tissues, you greatly grow your ability to 'hear' and receive the communications from all living creatures. You make new friends!

Native peoples of the Earth recognize that even the appearance of a certain animal or bird can have specific meaning for us. For example, hawks flying overhead can be a warning to pay attention. Other creatures can represent good fortune. Eventually, you can receive perhaps the most laudable prize of life to accomplish as a human — guidance from the Mind of the Energy of Life — through all creatures.

This is what Native peoples call:
'the-spirit-that-moves-through-all-things'.

You have struck Eco-Joy gold! By opening the communication channel to your Big Mind, you can now enter the jet stream current of UPLIFTING. Kudos!!!!

Of course, there's no guarantee that every tree, bird, flower or other species will want to talk to you, even when you beam them with your ENERGY JOY. That's their choice.

But... you are at least providing the medium for receiving and broadcasting. They might need repeated exposures to trust you. You might need practice to 'calibrate' better and accurately perceive their content.

Fantastic fun awaits!

35

THE ENERGY OF BLESSINGS AND BETTER

With an energy understanding, we now have a way of describing 'blessing' as the experience and the results of being bathed in higher frequencies of the Energy of Life. It 'blesses' you with connection — to the energy level source of life. That contact results in you being vastly uplifted into greater coherence. This means you can be a healthier, more functional part of a much larger whole, even if momentarily.

There are many benefits.

When you become more aligned with the energy level source of DNA, this 'awareness' — that has the original instructions for optimal health, healing and life — corrects things. This greater coherence aligns us energetically so things just get better, sometimes 'magically'.

The energy of joy excites our entire body/mind being at a human level like sunlight excites electrons of physical matter and briefly uplifts them into a higher energy realm. As they return to their former orbit, they release the newly gained energy which then fuels the 'work' of biological life.

'Better' means you are growing that energy into reality, into the quantum field of our biosphere. Our Earth Mother applauds and responds with even more 'better'. As a species we have no clue of how incredible living on Earth can become when we collaborate. We can literally create, grow and generate this type of positive response — this uplifting interchange of energy — into all we do, into everything and everyone.

> **This is how we uplift life on Earth. We use our energy together to energize good.**

Keep in mind that this is likely not going to be accomplished by people with the value system of survival. They are often the ones 'in charge' of human civilization at this time. Sadly, they cannot 'resonate' energetically with the Energy of Life enough to receive its guidance, even though it will usher in perhaps the single greatest true economic prosperity imaginable. It is invisible and without value to them.

Energetically, the values esteemed by survival dominate their perception. This locks the tuning of their HPA-axis into lower frequencies of awareness. So they literally block the Energy of Life from flowing because they're using the Law of Attraction to gain only a narrow band of frequencies — survival's lowest goals. Evolutionarily, it's like being stuck in energy quicksand.

These humans will eventually be considered the Neanderthals of UPLIFTING.

More conscious humans, those who choose to uplift, are evolving our species into its next stage. We are fertilizing physicality with the equivalent of energy seeds that sprout greater awareness, joy, health — all of which grow us 'up' — into the greater coherence of fuller oneness with the Mind of the Energy of Life. That is our direction of evolution.

This is THE journey that all true spiritual/religious/wisdom traditions are supposed to guide us along to evolve our awareness.

You can decide for yourself if yours is doing this job effectively.

Within all sacred texts around the world are allusions and direct writings stating this. You may find it fun to re-read such texts and begin to discover where and how these simple goals and concepts are touched upon. Through the ages, the purposes and the tools of these teachings have been sidelined, forgotten, purposefully obstructed, hidden, and abused.

Clearly, we went down the wrong rabbit hole. Fortunately, we can take the ENERGY JOY escalator all the way up.

As the top values of the U.S. Constitution and its governing principles, life, liberty and the pursuit of happiness have their energy level reality. ENERGY JOY is happiness of the energy realm. This also energizes life with energy health and frees us to live with our purpose ON.

As humans we thrive with the wealth of greater meaning when we live and walk with a higher purpose.

Your species level purpose is ON by turning on your ENERGY JOY engine so you are contributing energy to this amazing time of UPLIFTING the biosphere.

Your personal level purpose is also ON when you're following the 'yellow brick road' of guidance which you are using your ENERGY JOY to attract and connect with.

You become a being with purpose when you use your 'being' — your time, space, energy and focus — to be what you are and achieve why you are here.

As Isaac Bashevis Singer wittily put it (quoted by Rabbi Jonathan Sacks), *"We have to be free; we have no choice."*

36

SUPERCONDUCTIVE HUMANS

At physical levels, the more our brain neurons interconnect, the more intelligence we have. Like fungi networks under the soil connect and communicate with trees as a biological phone system, *We the People of the Earth* are growing an energy-linking flow of the Energy of Life into us, through us and into our biosphere. Everyone and everything can then bathe in it and can be uplifted. We become like energy rabbits spreading the highly contagious energy of joy.

Here's what we are accomplishing.

We are growing the energy source of joy into the biosphere until we are living in an atmosphere of ENERGY JOY. This is our gift to the world. It nourishes life.

The goal is to open the flow and to cease obstructing the flow so more of its uplifting communications are more available and increasingly present.

> **This is a way beyond and above the destructive survival level mentality permeating human civilization on Earth.**

While we do not know how many people are required to reach the tipping point, this is likely the fastest and most direct way to achieve the UPLIFTING.

What are we actually doing?

Biophysics calls this a 'macrophasic shift into greater coherence'. Evolutionarily we are being 'invited' — if not forced — to become healthy functioning parts of a greater whole. It's like a basketball team, a soccer team or a football team whose individual teammates are so aware of each other, so aware of every opportunity around them and so fully aligned with the goal of winning that they move together as a single organism.

> **Our species can become far more coherent while keeping our individuality and our freedoms intact.**

We are in a sense establishing a foundation for what physics calls 'superfluidity'. This is when all the molecules in physical matter move as one. **Like molecules, *We the People of the Earth* need to simply agree on one highest value that we all honor all the time.** When all our behaviors and institutions serve that value, especially if that value is the Prime Directive to nourish life, then our entire species and life on Earth, which we so powerfully impact, will uplift into greater health and joy.

It means in biophysics terms that random energy is channeled into coherent modes of activity that make living systems, which are by nature non-equilibrium and dynamic, more stable.[60]

Life on Earth right now is not stable. The climate changes are increasingly catastrophic. Dangers to human civilization grow as chaos is amplified.

Life on Earth is made unstable because of human incompetence to live in a life-nourishing way. More and more people around the world are recognizing we have no choice but to end the dysfunction of business as usual and create a healthy future.

The indigenous peoples of the Earth, who know our Earth Mother well, are concerned. They have lived in balance for millennia and know the benefits of living in respectful and loving partnership with Nature. Western civilizations have considered them as inferior or unsophisticated by judging through the lens that values business, finance, weaponry and technology — all applied as if life is a constant war to fight — not a wondrous and rare blessing to enjoy.

But indigenous peoples have the most valuable knowledge — the wisdom of living. They see those who are polluting the Earth for money and control as unbelievably ignorant of the most basic understanding of reality.

What is hopeful is that chaos in biological systems can go in either of two directions.

One results in disintegration, decay, illness and death. The energy in the system gets depleted — usually because the system is dysfunctional. It doesn't use its supply of energy efficiently, or the energy supply becomes insufficient and there's not enough stored energy to keep going. It doesn't regenerate energy. It dissolves.

Without swift and major changes, we are heading that direction.

Fortunately, there is also great opportunity in chaos. The more attractive direction is reorganizing into a greater whole of coherence we call growth.

What makes a chaotic biological system do a macrophasic shift into its greater whole?

Just as sunlight excites electrons to uplift, when energy is added to chaos, it can activate the healthier outcome of an upward shift into greater coherence.

> **ENERGY JOY is the excitatory electron for uplifting into healthier stability.**

This agreement to live in mutually nourishing collaboration with Nature can give us a human species-wide form of 'superconductivity'. In solid state physics, this is when electricity is conducted with zero resistance. This means knowledge, wisdom and new solutions that nourish life on Earth can be communicated easily — welcomed, funded and implemented into our civilization.

As a species, we should all want to know how to live better and better. At the very least, we always keep an eye open to whatever we do, and notice its impact on biological prosperity.

Such superconductivity does not mean that 'resistance is futile'. It reflects a maturity of our species to cooperate, collaborate and contribute to greater well-being throughout the biosphere.

What larger whole are we joining? We become partners with our beloved Earth Mother so we can receive more of the awareness of the Mind of the Energy of Life.

As we grow our understanding of 'being', we recognize our Earth Mother is the being that is this planet. And as we elevate up the evolutionary ladder of awareness, we recognize that the being that is our Earth Mother is far more conscious than are we.

> **She has the consciousness of an entire planet.**

As mentioned, one way wisdom traditions cultivated this more sophisticated awareness of biological intelligence was by making decisions based on how seven generations into the future would be affected.

Health and joy, which nourish life, are our elevators for uplifting. That is the direction our Earth Mother wants. She guides us to live best in this, her being.

We imagine the possibilities. We make them probable. We uplift.

37

CAN YOUR FOCUS COME OUT AND PLAY?

When you assess people's actions, goals and values in reference to the Prime Directive — to nourish life — and how well aligned they are with the highest values of health and joy, then you can easily see how far off base, how lost in physicality, how self-serving, how unaware — and therefore how destructive — are the human Enemies of Life.

Rudderless in reality, they seek power without wisdom or basic biological intelligence.

Enemies of Life have themselves become slaves to what is now a digital, virtual totem. But because it is without values, completely divorced from biological reality and does not even serve the Prime Directive, money has become an idiot idol, a buffoon dictator.

The real awareness comes through the heart. This is the main communication channel that the Mind of the Energy of Life uses. We can feel there what's right, true and good as well as what's not. There we can choose to sacrifice anger and fear for joy and love.

This is of the substance we call 'wisdom'. Wisdom flows more fully when we can place our awareness, our focus, in our heart 'center'. This opens the energy of the heart.

Like a physical lock and key mechanism, this energetic level gateway is opened by specific energy frequencies – those of joy and love. With your Energy Heart beaming, you're holding open, wider and wider, the gateway to what has poetically and metaphorically been called: the 'Divine spark' and the 'kingdom of heaven within'.

These names, whether from spiritual or religious traditions, were trying to describe three important clues:

1. the **'what'** – the actual non-physical yet real and spectacular substance
2. the **'where'** – the location to place our focus to find this substance
3. the **'why'** – the value that compared to all else is considered 'heavenly' and 'divine'

There's only one additional ingredient needed to put these clues together.

4. the **'how'** – to advance and best operate your ENERGY JOY engine

Fortunately, and amazingly, there is an ancient three-step secret formula.

38

TRUE HOLINESS

The Ancient Energy Formula

While you now have a practical technique to turn on your ENERGY JOY engine, for over 3500 years we have always been provided with a 'magical' three-element, reality-enhancing tool to uplift life on Earth. This simple formula exponentially expands our human awareness and our capacity to cherish life. It does much more.

However, also for the past 3500 years, with rare and wonderful exceptions, very few humans have been able to figure out this formula. Now with bio-physics we can begin to understand this formula better and recognize the urgent need for invoking it. While folklore tells us that "necessity is the mother of invention," ancient wisdom recommends that to make good use of this principle, we must 'increase our necessity'.

This is now our current situation. We have major uplifting to do.

> **To access the very best energy, we move our focus upstream — as high as we can.**

If you seek an inspiring experience, imagine the energy of true holiness — the real thing. What does that mean to you? What does 'holy' mean to you?

Being 'holy' means it functions in the uplifting ways that serve to connect you, stabilize you and immerse you in the Energy of Life — enough to perceive the Mind of the Energy of Life and the presence of the BEING that is Reality.

There has always been a highly effective focusing tool that helps achieve this goal.

With an ENERGY understanding — NOT a religious and NOT a spiritual perspective — we can now describe, understand and utilize this most brilliant application of focusing for our ultimate evolutionary advancement.

Science Meets Ancient Wisdom – The Formula

"Love your god with all your heart". [61,62]

1. *"Love"* is the most powerful energy of our emotional level.

It is the prize of life. Now we can begin to comprehend some of its higher level functions. Recall the definition of emotion as "energy in motion". Hints of its power have come to us via popular music, exalting love as "what makes the world go around" and that "love is all we need". In his famous Riverside speech, Martin Luther King, Jr. realized love's fullness as a force identical to what wisdom traditions say: "Human love is but the lowest form of real love." [63] In Genesis, the Torah (which translates from Hebrew as "Teaching") states that the entire Creation was created out of 'love'.

While we don't understand that depth, the creative life force and love are one. **We are all beings who are being loved into being — continuously. We're not hated into being.**

Understanding this energetically as bio-physics, we can acknowledge that its opposite — hating — contaminates the quantum field of reality and uncouples the hater from the Mind of the Energy of Life. With your ENERGY JOY engine turned on, you can grow the energy which gives love its life and power.

2. *"Your god"* is where we aim love's energy.

It's how we best direct our energy altogether. What's absolutely vital is to read this correctly as YOUR god, not someone else's version, nor whatever religions, institutions, parents, schools and books have declared as 'The Creator'. It's about elevating YOU.

> **To direct the powerful energy of love, we focus our own mind on whatever is — for us — THE highest, most benevolent, absolutely supreme, unconditionally loving and most divine concept we ourselves can imagine.**

At a practical level of energy use, we are raising the frequency of our focus, which directs energy and delivers content. We stretch and grow our mind — with energy.

In other words, the formula is to connect these two dots of:
a) the most powerful emotional energy of love with
b) the highest frequencies of mental energy

> **By thinking at the peak of our best imaginings, we are in effect powering our awareness into new realms. This is an amazing evolutionary tool!**

We are also consciously and continuously growing our capacities. This ancient formula's gifts are unlimited in that it connects us with more and more of the BEING that is Reality.

3. *"With all your heart"* tells us two important pieces of this formula.

First is WHERE to focus to activate this energy engine. We focus physically in the center of our chest, the heart area. Why? This location is where ancient sages have known to find the 'valve' that opens the flow of ENERGY JOY by whatever name. Our Energy Heart is there patiently awaiting our discovery and activation.

Second, the word 'all' is important because it is not limited to the heart's emotional level of love. This opens the door for including the heart's energy level of love.

Together, these three components turn on the ENERGY JOY engine and activate its flow.

> **Doing this daily for even a couple of minutes gives you the most potent mind expansion imaginable!**

Greediness for more and more is destructive here like it is everywhere in the physical realm. Little by little is the healthy way. This is because you want to build up your neural pathways so they are strong enough to handle your expansion. More than a few minutes at a time with this powerful focus is not needed. We get what we are meant to experience and we learn along the way by building a good foundation. You don't want a 'short cut' or a 'fast track' because that means you'll have skipped essential components. Your results won't be stable or reliable. You won't get 'there' that way.

Let's summarize

Applying the combination of Dynamic Calm's treasures

Presence of Mind
Emotional Calm
Inner Peace and
Physical Relation
with
Genius Focus and ENERGY JOY, you can take it easy, relax and enjoy the ride of a lifetime into your uplifting — with full confidence that by doing so you are contributing to THE UPLIFTING of all life on Earth.

By radiating ENERGY JOY, which is uplifting by itself, you are also infusing the consciousness of the Mind of the Energy of Life into the fabric of our biosphere.

When you add the ancient energy formula for "True Holiness", you uplift big time.

That is how we can elevate our fellow humans out of the mentality of survival into the grander consciousness of UPLIFTING — our species' job and greatest contribution.

If... this is indeed how *We the People of the Earth* can activate UPLIFTING, then we have a most delightful and fascinating adventure to focus on co-creating together — starting NOW — during our lifetime.

Why delay?

The sooner we begin, the more we can experience while we are living.

39

ENERGY JOY CULTURE

Uplifting Together

Everything is energy. But all energy is not the same.

We have to get smart about energy. Whether we use it wisely or not, we are impacting life on Earth. Eventually, *We the People of the Earth* have to responsibly choose the direction we want to grow.

Why not now?

Otherwise, it will continue to be chosen for us by Enemies of Life, those rather unevolved humans lacking biological intelligence, who are ruled by the inferior values of basic survival — now dangerously dysfunctional — which only eradicate the best moral and ethical standards of humanity.

We are not here as a species to be victims of such ignorance.

> **We choose our direction — and the actual reality we create on Earth — by establishing globally the very top value we most want that functions energetically to nourish life. *We the People of the Earth* need to simply agree on this one highest value that we ALL honor – ALL the time.**

Our dominant value is what transforms our life energy into creating all its downstream forms — our beliefs, our thoughts, our feelings, our behaviors, our relationships, our desires, our intentions and... our awareness. This is how an 'energy value' expresses itself in the living energy matrix of our Earth Mother's generous biosphere.

As our top 'energy value' continues its expression into physicality, we eventually affect more and more of the physical — our bodies and the environment. We grow the reality we want.

> **As a species, our job is to operate this process globally to grow health and joy.**

Our power comes with recognizing that we are in an 'energy communication medium', the living energy matrix of our Earth Mother. Perhaps we can more easily relate to this as our Earth Mother's 'Mind' or her 'Soul'. As we focus with the energy of this top value, we communicate what we want MORE OF to this amazing Being that is our Earth Mother. Applying knowledge of bio-physics, we use our focus to direct energy that delivers, infused into it, the content we want MORE OF.

Let's start communicating the joys of life to this living energy matrix and stop communicating the fears of survival. Doing so includes changing media, entertainment and politics to promote our top value and educate our fellow humans well. We stop promoting violence, killing, destruction and cruelty.

> **Our Earth Mother grows things. So... if we want to uplift, we go upstream to have greatest leverage with our top value.**

This frees us from non-stop micro-managing all our thoughts, feelings, behavior and awareness — and then trying endlessly to convince and coerce others to listen to us.

If everyone is aligned with the top values of health and joy, committed to nourishing life on Earth, then it doesn't matter which political 'party' is in charge because we are all on the same side, working together for the same top goals.

Instead of hating and killing over our differences, we choose to welcome and enjoy sharing our species' best achievements with each other. Like a new Olympics, we celebrate and honor the unique contributions each culture and each peoples bring to uplifting the human experience.

Let's have more fun! Let's grow fun into our reality!

To get this process jump-started and activate UPLIFTING, we each turn on our personal ENERGY JOY engine and learn how to open its energy flow more and more. This is also because:

> **We blossom each other! The ENERGY JOY you develop and radiate naturally helps activate the ENERGY JOY engine in others to turn on and open its flow in them. We blossom each other.**

Once your ENERGY JOY engine is on, you can create joy wherever you go. You are fertilizing the biosphere with the elevating Energy of Life and and pollinating Earth's energy atmosphere with its uplifting awareness.

YOU are uplifting — yourself, others and the biosphere.

This is how you join the UPLIFTING. Like a secret handshake, we greet, welcome and celebrate each other with ENERGY JOY. Others engaged in UPLIFTING recognize you by your energy.

Quite important is that in addition, you are helping to prevent other species from pulling the trigger on deciding to rid the Earth of us dangerous humans.

At this point, we have to PROVE to them that we are conscious enough to value the preciousness of life on this, our wondrous alive planet, and that we want to join the community of Earth's living beings as a contributing member.

How do we convince them?

We tune up what we are broadcasting with our energy.

All the other species can feel energy far better than we and in many more ways. Your energy broadcasts out your thoughts, your emotions and your intentions. You cannot fool these more energy-aware living beings. This is why they all flee from us in Nature. They don't run to us to play.

To convince them that we are capable of changing and maturing — telling them we want to contribute value to Earth's community of living beings — we need to very quickly start beaming ENERGY JOY to them. We want them to stop considering us as a dysfunctional, selfish, destructive, negative force that has no respect for their habitats, nor the life quality of anything or anyone, including ourselves.

We are not a highly regarded species.

One rather subtle way our Earth Mother can rid her surface of humans is simply to put into the dysfunctional minds of Enemies of Life new types of lethal biological weapons that spread disease uncontrollably and kill vast numbers of people. The makers of these weapons may imagine they are clever inventors who will make more money and triumph, but they are no match for her greater Mind. It would seem this has already begun.

Fortunately, ENERGY JOY is something real other species can feel. It tells them that our energy heart has finally opened and is activating.

> **ENERGY JOY is the energy language of all living things.**

Most generously, they have been waiting ever so patiently with faith in us.

> **You can start uplifting your personal life in a zillion, creative ways by being an ENERGY JOY Beamer!**

For example, you can intentionally 'beam' ENERGY JOY to the people in your life, as well as in the places you are and at the events you engage. Hugging someone with your ENERGY JOY engine humming is a new, improved super quantum hug! When both people can do this, the synergy uplifts you both enormously.

Since this energy is not limited by physical space, you can also beam people over the phone and infuse ENERGY JOY into your virtual life online. You can beam people across the room from you. You can beam people all around the world just by turning on your ENERGY JOY engine and thinking of them.

Imagine starting every business meeting with an inspiring abundance of team-generated ENERGY JOY filling the room with positivity, that also opens everyone's access to creativity and brilliant solutions. This is how businesses will flourish – by innovating the valued new products, goods and services that nourish life with health and joy.

People everywhere want to have meaningful work they can engage in with real purpose. Genuinely improving life on Earth is such a worthy quest.

Since this energy is also not limited by time, this means you can even beam ENERGY JOY into any future event you want — like a date, a meeting, a restaurant, a musical concert or any gathering — to uplift those experiences for everyone.

Doing so gives you a way to recognize how your positive influence is blossoming.

To accelerate even more, we can join together in ENERGY JOY groups to greatly uplift each other. We beam better together!

As more and more of us do this, everything starts uplifting. Bigger, better fun begins!

Utilizing this energy to raise the consciousness of our entire species, these are ways for how we grow ENERGY JOY to reach the tipping point that elevates humanity out of survival into uplifting.

Let's do this together — quietly, benevolently, confidently, playfully, artfully — and purposefully have some outrageous joy.

I shall love hearing of your successes.

Our wondrous UPLIFTING adventure is calling!

Our Earth Mother grows things!

We can grow anything we want

into our biological reality.

Let's choose to make

life on Earth healthy fun!

APPENDIX

Not a call to arms, or legs,

ENERGY JOY

is a call to heart.

References

1 Swimme, Brian; Berry, Thomas, *The Universe Story: From the Primordial Flaring Forth to the Ecozoic Era, A Celebration of the Unfolding of the Cosmos,* HarperSanFrancisco, 1992.

2 Ho, Mae-Wan: *The Rainbow and The Worm: The Physics of Organisms,* 2nd Edition, World Scientific Publishing Co. Pte., Ltd., Singapore, 1998.

3 Aditi Nerurkar et al. *"When Physicians Counsel About Stress: Results of a National Study,"* JAMA Internal Medicine. 2013;173(1):76-77. doi:10.1001/2013.jamainternmed.480

4 Perkins, A. (1994). *Saving money by reducing stress.* Harvard Business Review. 72(6):12.

5 *American Institute of Stress*

6 *European Agency for Safety & Health – study of USA workers,* NIOSH

7 *Journal of Occupational & Environmental Medicine,* NIOSH

8 Hight, Cathi, *Institute,* US Chamber of Commerce Foundation, 2012 (blog)

9 Siegel, Robert Simon, *The Stress Fix: Future Wellness Producing Healthy People*, training manual, 2019.

10 ibid.

11 Guilliams, Thomas G., Ph.D., *The Role of Stress and the HPA Axis in Chronic Disease Management,* Point Institute, 2018.

12 Aditi Nerurkar et al. *"When Physicians Counsel About Stress: Results of a National Study,"* JAMA Internal Medicine. 2013;173(1):76-77. doi:10.1001/2013.jamainternmed.480

13 Perkins, A. (1994). *Saving money by reducing stress.* Harvard Business Review. 72(6):12.

14 *European Agency for Safety & Health – study of USA workers,* NIOSH

15 Guilliams, Thomas G., Ph.D., *The Role of Stress and the HPA Axis in Chronic Disease Management,* Point Institute, 2018.

16 ibid.

17 Rosch, Paul J., MD. editor, *Bioelectromagnetic and Subtle Energy Medicine,* CRC Press, Taylor & Francis Group, Boca Raton, FL., 2015.

18 Presman, A.S. *Electromagnetic Fields and Life,* Plenum Press, New York, 1970. In Ho, Mae-Wan: *The Rainbow and The Worm: The Physics of Organisms,* 2nd Edition, World Scientific Publishing Co. Pte., Ltd., Singapore, 1998.

19 Lipton, Bruce, H. Ph.D., *The Biology of Belief,* Hay House, Inc., Carlsbad, California, 2005, 2015.

20 Hardell, Lennart; Nyberg, Rainer, *Appeals that matter or not on a moratorium on the deployment of the fifth generation, 5G, for microwave radiation, Molecular and Clinical Oncology,* January 2020.

21 Hawken, Paul; Lovins, Amory; Lovins, Hinter L., *Natural Capitalism,* Little Brown & Company, NY, 1999.

22 Hawken, Paul, *Regeneration: Ending the Climate Crisis in One Generation,* Penguin Books, NY, 2021.

23 Sapolsky, Robert M., *Why Zebras Don't Get Ulcers,* Henry Holt and Company, NY, 2004.

24 ibid.

25 Guilliams, Thomas G., Ph.D., *The Role of Stress and the HPA Axis in Chronic Disease Management,* Point Institute, 2018.

26 ibid.

27 ibid.

28 ibid.

29 McKenna, Terence, *Food of the G-ds: The Search for the Original Tree of Knowledge,* Bantam Books, NY, 1993.

30 Swimme, Brian; Berry, Thomas, *The Universe Story: From the Primordial Flaring Forth to the Ecozoic Era, A Celebration of the Unfolding of the Cosmos,* HarperSanFrancisco, 1992.

31 Fraser, Peter H., Massey, H., Wilcox, Joan Parisi, *Decoding the Human Body-Field: The New Science of Information as Medicine,* Healing Arts Press, Rochester, Vermont, 2008.

32 Fraser, Peter, H., *Energy and Information in Nature,* Choice Point Communications, Poole, United Kingdom, 2012.

33 Miller GA. *The magical number seven, plus or minus two: some limits on our capacity for processing information,* Psychol Rev. 1956 Mar; 63(2):81-97.

34 Wolff, Milo, Schrodinger's Universe: *Einstein, Waves & the Origin of the Natural Laws,* Outskirts Press, Parker, CO, 2008.

35 Popp, F.A.. and Li, K.H. "Hyperbolic Relaxation as a Sufficient Condition of a Fully Coherent Ergodic Field. International Journal of Theoretical Physics, 32 (1993): 1573-1583.

36 Solomon, GF; Kay N.; Morley, JE; *Endorphins:A link between stress,emotions, immunity, and disease,* In Plotnikoff NP, Faith RE, Murgo AJ, et al (Eds): *Enkephalins and Endorphins,* New York, Plenum Press, 1986, 129-144.

37 Kiecolt-Glaser J, Glaser R: *Psychological influences on immunity.* Psychosomatics1986, Sep;27:621-624.

38 Pert, Candace B, Ph.D., *Molecules of Emotions,* Touchtone, NY, 1999.

39 Hawken, Paul, *Regeneration: Ending the Climate Crisis in One Generation,* Penguin Random House, 2021.

40 Kaufman, Frederick, *The Money Plot: A History of Currency's Power to Enchant, Control and Manipulate,* Other Press, NY, 2020.

41 F.A. Popp, W Nagl, K H Li, W Scholz, O Weingärtner, R Wolf *Biophoton emission. New evidence for coherence and DNA as source,* Cell Biophysiology, 1984 Mar;6(1):33-52.

42 Svent-Gyorgi, A. *Light and Life,* McElroy, W.D. and Glass, B., Eds., Johns Hopkins Press, Baltimore, 1961. In Ho, Mae-Wan: *The Rainbow and The Worm: The Physics of Organisms,* 2nd Edition, World Scientific Publishing Co. Pte., Ltd., Singapore, 1998.

43 ibid.

44 Christofferson, Travis, *Tripping Over the Truth,* Create Space Independent Publishing Platform, North Charleston, S.C., 2014.

45 Mercola, Joseph, MD. *Fat for Fuel: A Revolutionary Diet to Combat Cancer, Boost Brain Power and Increase Your Energy,* Hay House Inc. 2017.

46 Know, Lee, ND, *Mitochondria and the Future of Medicine: The Key to Understanding Disease, Chronic Illness, Aging and Life Itself,* Chelsea Green Publishing, Whte River Junction, Vermont, 2018.

47 Ho, Mae-Wan: *The Rainbow and The Worm: The Physics of Organisms,* 2nd Edition, World Scientific Publishing Co. Pte., Ltd., Singapore, 1998.

48 Becker, Robert O., MD, Cross Currents: The Promise of Electromedicine, The Perils of Electropollution, Jeremy P. Tarcher/Putnam, New York, 1990.

49 Becker, Robert O., MD, Selden, Gary, *Electromagnetism and The Foundation of Life,* Quill, Willian Morrow, 1985.

50 Scherman Nosson, Rabbi and Zlotowitz, Meir, Rabbi, General Editors, *The Chumash,* The Stone Edition, ArtScroll Series, Mesorah Publications, Ltd., NY, 1998, 2000.

51 https://www.resonancescience.org/blog/Supermassive-Black-Holes-Birthing-Stars-at-Furious-Rate?fbclid=IwAR0GJwx-XVq7QabuwBj4e8t-IJyOPo-YgKPMgtGx-UWHM6cpIkvzrxYJZUM

52 Ho, Mae-Wan: *The Rainbow and The Worm: The Physics of Organisms,* 2nd Edition, World Scientific Publishing Co. Pte., Ltd., Singapore, 1998.

53 Samuel Milham, MD, MPH, L. Lloyd Morgan, BS. A New Electromagnetic Exposure Metric: High Frequency Voltage Transients Associated With Increased Cancer Incidence in Teachers in a California School, American Journal of Industrial Medicine, 51(8):579-586, August 2008.

54 Campbell, W. H., 2003. *Introduction to Geomagnetic Fields* (2nd Ed). Cambridge University Press.

55 Popp, F.A. and Cohen, S. *Biophoton emissions in the human body,* Journal of Photochemistry and Photobiology B: Biology, 1997, 40: 187-9.

56 Dalai Lama, Desmond Tutu, Douglas Abrams, *The Book of Joy: Lasting Happiness in a Changing World,* Avery, Penguin Random House, New York, 2016.

57 Ho, Mae-Wan: *The Rainbow and The Worm: The Physics of Organisms,* 2nd Edition, World Scientific Publishing Co. Pte., Ltd., Singapore, 1998.

58 Hawken, Paul, *Regeneration: Ending the Climate Crisis in One Generation,* Penguin Random House, 2021.

59 https://www.resonancescience.org/blog/Supermassive-Black-Holes-Birthing-Stars-at-Furious-Rate?fbclid=IwAR0GJwx-XVq7QabuwBj4e8t-IJyOPo-YgKPMgtGx-UWHM6cpIkvzrxYJZUM

60 Ho, Mae-Wan: *The Rainbow and The Worm: The Physics of Organisms,* 2nd Edition, World Scientific Publishing Co. Pte., Ltd., Singapore, 1998.

61 In Genesis, Scherman Nosson, Rabbi and Zlotowitz, Meir, Rabbi, General Editors, *The Chumash,* The Stone Edition, ArtScroll Series, Mesorah Publications, Ltd., NY, 1998, 2000.

62 Miller, Rabbi Chaim (editor), *Torah: The Five Books of Moses,* The Slager Edition, Gutnick Library of Jewish Classics, Lifestyle Books, Brooklyn, NY, 2011.

63 Shah, Idries, *The Dermis Probe,* The Octagon Press, London, 1970, 1980.

Acknowlegements

Many wonderful people inspired me throughout writing this book, most without knowing of their contributions.

As a screenwriter, artist and more, my cousin Sally Park Rubin jumped in with initial editing brilliance. She, Ed and their talented son Sam are bright lights.

Kevin Walters' extreme generosity, kindness and consistent thoughtfulness over many years enabled me to survive through a metaphorical desert. Without his friendship and support, this book could not have been written.

As my nieces and nephews mature into adulthood, it is a treasure of joy to grow friendships with them all.

My niece Maiann Good is a delight in my life with our precious opportunities to talk at higher levels of consciousness with ease, understanding, shared perspective, encouragement and mutual appreciation.

My nephew Tommy Siegel's continuous blossoming of pure creativity inspires me through his music and his cartoon books of perverted perspective on birds, millennial life and stuff.

My nephew Andrew Breton's detailed suggestions of my initial manuscript were greatly appreciated.

My niece Julia Siegel-Breton's natural grace and achievements are a special source of joy and pride.

In my spiritual life, I've had many influences to learn from. I'll mention only the good ones. My spiritual foundation was built since my twenties from the supremely functional writings of Idries Shah. His extraordinary and multi-dimensionally precise use of language informs and inspires.

I am very grateful for my friend Rabbi Dovid Fredman, who single-handedly re-connected me with Judaism and sources of its ancient wisdom. He, the Seattle Kollel and delicious Shabbat dinners his wife Giti prepared gave full spectrum nourishment.

Yehuda Frankl, my friend and Yeshiva scholar, engaged my mind and spirit with our years of late night discussions, studying texts together and sharing of his immense knowledge with his contagious joy. I want to thank Rabbi Dovid Asher for involving me in the programs to meet Yehuda as well as his kindnesses to my Mom and for his scholarly knowledge of Judaism.

I am grateful for all my friends at Chabad and for the delicious dinners Nechomi prepared. Special thanks to Yael, Yohanatan, Marty and Yossi.

More recently, Dr. Vladmir Zelenko's medical brilliance and sparkling clarity in his book *Essence to Essence* have demonstrated his exceptionalism, humanity and courageous dedication to truth.

Hanging out with my friend Iron Eagle, Frank Sanchez, seventh generation treaty signer, Sundance Priest and former Chief of the Nakota Nation, whom many consider a holy person, has given me immense joy and unique affirmation.

I am also grateful to Juliana Tan, perhaps the most amazingly talented healer, clairvoyant and spiritual warrior I have met. The work she does is life-saving and beyond compare. Our unique friendship is most valued.

In today's rarified world of truth-telling in science and health, my inspiration grows from the brilliant and courageous physicians of FLCCC and Dr. Joseph Mercola, who have pioneered medical truth during the pandemic, from the solid foundation of genuine patriotism of Robert Kennedy Jr. with his team at Children's Health Defense and from Del Bigtree with his ever-refreshing news program at TheHighwire.com and the brilliant legal achievements of ICAN.

My favorite and most influential authors in the science of biophysics are Milo Wolf *(Shroedinger's Universe)* and Mae Won Ho *(The Rainbow and The Worm)*.

This book, and all of my work over the past two decades, have been made visually beautiful and highly professional by the wondrous talent and sensitivity of my dear friend Anita Williams, graphic designer extraordinaire. Thank you Anita, for all your gifts!

Finally, to HaShem for all that is, was and will be love.

About the Author

Robert Simon Siegel, MS brings a traditional wisdom understanding of 'energy' into science and physiology to achieve new levels of health, joy and biological intelligence now needed to uplift from pandemic malaise. With three decades of clinical experience as a stress specialist in medical centers and companies, Robert developed these educational tools by uniting science and his personal trainings with wisdom tradition lineage-holders.

Robert's clients have included CEOs of multi-national corporations, a sitting Governor, police chief, physicians, nurses and people from all walks of life. His client organizations have included: Chevron, USA, NBC, Providence Health Systems, Port of Seattle Police Dept., King County WA, Washington Athletic Club, TRW and Pritikin Longevity Center.

His articles have appeared in *CAPITAL: Business & Finance Magazine* (Middle Eastern edition), the *Washington Athletic Club Magazine, Workers Compensation Monthly* and *QI: The Journal of Eastern Health & Fitness*. The New England Hospital Assembly honored the stress unit he directed at Mt. Pleasant Hospital. Twice a selected speaker at the National Wellness Conference, Robert presented "Fixing Stress" panel at the 2015 *Health and Productivity Forum* for Integrated Benefits Institute.

HOW TO LEARN ENERGY JOY – THE STRESS FIX

Individuals and organizations can enjoy gaining these skills online via TheStressFix.com. For live trainings, talks and private sessions, please contact Robert at: info@TheStressFix.com.

www.TheStressFix.com